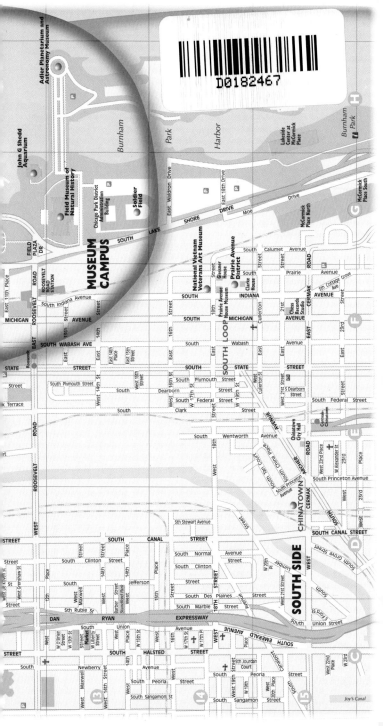

CITYPACK TOP 25
Chicago

MICK SINCLAIR
ADDITIONAL WRITING BY ELAINE GLUSAC

AA Publishing
If you have any comments or suggestions for this guide you can contact the editor at
travelguides@TheAA.com

How to Use This Book

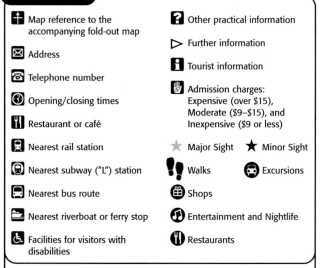

KEY TO SYMBOLS

- ✚ Map reference to the accompanying fold-out map
- ✉ Address
- ☎ Telephone number
- ⏱ Opening/closing times
- 🍴 Restaurant or café
- 🚆 Nearest rail station
- Ⓛ Nearest subway ("L") station
- 🚌 Nearest bus route
- ⛴ Nearest riverboat or ferry stop
- ♿ Facilities for visitors with disabilities

- ❓ Other practical information
- ▷ Further information
- ℹ Tourist information
- ✋ Admission charges: Expensive (over $15), Moderate ($9–$15), and Inexpensive ($9 or less)
- ★ Major Sight
- ★ Minor Sight
- 👣 Walks
- 🚍 Excursions
- 🛍 Shops
- 🎭 Entertainment and Nightlife
- 🍴 Restaurants

This guide is divided into four sections

- Essential Chicago: An introduction to the city and tips on making the most of your stay.
- Chicago by Area: We've broken the city into five areas, and recommended the best sights, shops, entertainment venues, nightlife and restaurants in each one. Suggested walks help you to explore on foot.
- Where to Stay: The best hotels, whether you're looking for luxury, budget or something in between.
- Need to Know: The info you need to make your trip run smoothly, including getting about by public transportation, weather tips, emergency phone numbers and useful websites.

Navigation In the Chicago by Area chapter, we've given each area its own color, which is also used on the locator maps throughout the book and the map on the inside front cover.

Maps The fold-out map accompanying this book is a comprehensive street plan of Chicago. The grid on this fold-out map is the same as the grid on the locator maps within the book. We've given grid references within the book for each sight and listing.

Contents

Introducing Chicago

Poet Carl Sandburg called it "City of the big shoulders." Mayor Richard J. Daley boasts it's "the city that works." Pick your interpretation—city of brawn and industry, brash and bustling, modern and innovative—it's all here in Chicago.

The unofficial capital of the Midwest, Chicago earned the moniker "Second City" for trailing New York in size. But Chicago never played the scripted stepchild. From the beginnings, a distinct breed of entrepreneurs and hucksters made their way to the city's Lake Michigan shores seeking opportunity. No amount of tragedy could persuade them from their enterprises, be they legal or not. Two days after the Great Chicago Fire of 1871 had reduced most of the city to ashes, one real-estate broker posted a sign reading: "All gone but wife, children and energy."

Afterward, the city shucked its 19th-century past and became the most modern metropolis in the country, if not the world, home to the first skyscraper and a new Prairie School of architecture in sync with the low, limitless horizon of the region. Musicians came and amped up the blues. Gangsters grabbed a piece of the action and held on. Everyone thought big. "Make no little plans," said former Chicago city planner and architect Daniel Burnham, "they have no magic to stir men's blood."

The spirit of optimism that marks the commercial aspects of the city is distinct on a personal level, too. It's a common stereotype that Midwesterners are friendly; Chicagoans are often that and much more—honest, opinionated and curious. It takes optimism to emigrate and Chicago received wave after wave of Scandinavians and Germans early on, and still welcomes incoming Irish, Polish, Mexicans and Filipinos.

Chicago is perhaps the most American city of all.

Facts + Figures

- **Residents: 2.9 million**
- **Languages spoken: 132**
- **Museums: 70**
- **Parks: 552**
- **Ranking: 3rd-largest city in the US**
- **Lakefront bike paths: 18 miles (29km)**

MUSICAL CHICAGO

Jazz has thrived in the city since the 1920s when New Orleans' innovators moved north. Louis Armstrong struck out on his own with the "Hot Five" recordings he made in town. Later, African-Americans moving up from the rural South settled in and took the traditional blues music electric. Both jazz and blues clubs still entertain today.

EDIBLE CHICAGO

In the early 20th century Chicago was a meat-and-potatoes town, home of stock-yards and slaughterhouses and the railroad hub transporting beef to the outer regions. Steak houses, deep-dish pizza and hot dogs continue the tradition of substantive eating in Chicago. But in the past 25 years the city has nurtured a modern band of chefs to become one of the most innovative places to eat in the US.

DESIGN CHICAGO

Architects and entrepreneurs engineered Chicago's phoenix after the Great Fire, inventing the skyscraper in the rebuilding. Daniel Burnham had bold plans for Chicago's front yard of parks that buffer city and shore. Frank Lloyd Wright founded his Prairie School of design here. Later innovators such as Mies van der Rohe also left their mark and bolstered Chicago's reputation as a great architectural town.

A Short Stay in Chicago

DAY 1

Morning Start your stay with a 9am stroll around **Millennium Park** (▷ 50) downtown, to walk across Frank Gehry's bridge and photograph the reflections on the highly polished bean-shape sculpture by Anish Kapoor.

Mid-morning Walk the two blocks over to the **Art Institute of Chicago** (▷ 44). Doors open at 10.30 most days, 10 on weekends, and lines form at least 15 minutes prior. It's worth the effort to have the Impressionist galleries briefly to yourself.

Lunch Take a break and soak up the Loop atmosphere at **Atwood Café** (▷ 37), just a few blocks northwest of the museum on Washington and State streets.

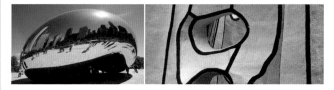

Afternoon Head to Randolph and Wabash, where you can catch the elevated train, aka the **El** (▷ 26). Take the Brown Line bound for Kimball. Get off at the Belmont stop and walk to the opposite platform to catch the train heading back to the Loop.

Mid-afternoon Take a walk around the **Loop** to admire some public sculpture installed there (▷ 25). Start with the unnamed Picasso in Daley Center Plaza then go to the Calder at the Federal Center Plaza and the Jean Dubuffet at the James R. Thompson Center.

Dinner Head for **Gino's East** (▷ panel, 80) for an authentic taste of Chicago's deep-dish pizza.

Evening Get tickets to **Second City** (▷ 67) for a good guffaw over Chicago-style humor, which is topical and partly improvised.

DAY 2

Morning Hop on the 10am **Architecture Foundation River Cruise** (▷ 24) offered by the Chicago Architecture Foundation. The tours are a big draw and usually sell out so plan ahead and reserve before coming to town.

Mid-morning Disembark the boat and walk up the **Magnificent Mile** (▷ 68), the stretch of Michigan Avenue that runs from the Chicago River up to Oak Street, to check out the tony shopping district and a number of architectural landmarks including the **Wrigley Building** (▷ 72), **Tribune Tower** (▷ 72) and the John Hancock Center.

Lunch Stop for lunch at the **Museum of Contemporary Art** (▷ 71), where the celebrated Austrian-turned-Californian chef Wolfgang Puck runs a café in a sunny, art-filled space.

Afternoon Rent bikes at **Navy Pier** (▷ 64) and take a spin on the Lake Michigan shoreline past the popular **Oak Street** (▷ 71) and **North Avenue** (▷ 66) beaches to appreciate how Chicagoans play.

Mid-afternoon Ascend the **John Hancock Center** (▷ 60) to the Observatory to see Chicago from 1,000ft (305m) above the ground.

Dinner Sit down to order a sampling of wine perfectly paired to entrées as well as small, shareable plates at the innovative wine bar and café **Bin 36** (▷ 79).

Evening Take a cab to **Buddy Guy's Legends** (▷ 86) on the near South Side to catch a few sets of the blues before calling it a night.

Top 25

These pages are a quick guide to the Top 25, which are described in more detail later. Here they are listed alphabetically and the tinted background shows the area they are in.

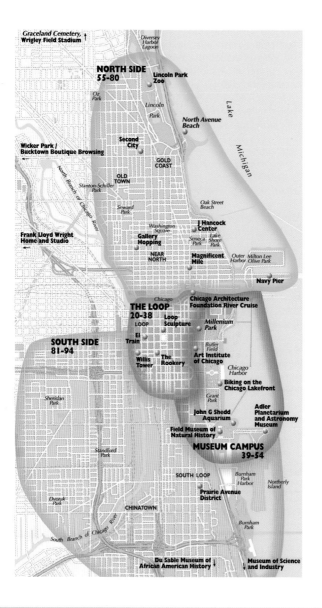

Graceland Cemetery,
Wrigley Field Stadium

Diversey
Harbor
Lagoon

NORTH SIDE
55-80

Lincoln Park
Zoo

Oz
Park

Lincoln
Park

North Avenue
Beach

Wicker Park /
Bucktown Boutique Browsing

Second
City

North Branch of Chicago River

Stanton-Schiller
Park

**OLD
TOWN**

**GOLD
COAST**

Lake Michigan

Seward
Park

Oak Street
Beach

Frank Lloyd Wright
Home and Studio

Washington
Square

Gallery
Hopping

Hancock
Center

Seneca
Park

Lake
Shore
Park

**NEAR
NORTH**

Magnificent
Mile

Outer
Harbor

Milton Lee
Olive Park

Navy Pier

Chicago
River

Chicago Architecture
Foundation River Cruise

THE LOOP
20-38

LOOP

Loop
Sculpture

Millenium
Park

El
Train

Butler
Field

SOUTH SIDE
81-94

Sheridan
Park

Willis
Tower

The
Rookery

Art Institute
of Chicago

Chicago
Harbor

Biking on the
Chicago Lakefront

Grant
Park

Standford
Park

John G Shedd
Aquarium

Adler
Planetarium
and Astronomy
Museum

Field Museum of
Natural History

MUSEUM CAMPUS
39-54

Dvorak
Park

SOUTH LOOP

Burnham
Park Harbor

Northerly
Island

Prairie Avenue
District

CHINATOWN

Burnham
Park

South Branch of Chicago River

Du Sable Museum of
African American History

Museum of Science
and Industry

Shopping

Chicago's shops can excite the purchasing passions of the entire Midwest while surprising and delighting visitors from much farther afield. The upscale malls and boutiques on and around the Magnificent Mile attest to the international nature of the city, while the plethora of smaller independent outlets show that the city has retained its own character against the onslaught of globalized retailing.

Shopping Streets

For designer clothing, the Magnificent Mile is the showplace of Chicago. Men and women in pursuit of quality attire will find most major names represented in the high-rise malls along Michigan Avenue. For those who prefer a more personal shopping experience, a stroll around nearby Oak Street finds a clutch of elegant boutiques offering European haute couture and eager assistants. The same area hosts many of the city's major art galleries and antiques dealers.

Antiques and Retro

More fine art and antiques dealers can be found in River North, while their brasher, funkier counterparts are a feature in the shopping districts of Lake View and Wicker Park. There is also an abundance of outlets for extreme clothing, new and vintage, and bizarre household furnishings, often made by local craftspeople.

THE LOOP

Historic department stores such as Carson Pirie Scott (now the Sullivan Center) and Marshall Field's, now a Macy's, are reminders of the glory days of the Loop, when it was the social hub of the city. With the population and retail shift to suburbia, the Loop became solely a place of work, symbolized by its high-rise office towers. Aided by a 1990s rejuvenation that saw 1920s-style lampposts and subway entrances appear, the Loop has enjoyed a revival.

Chicago's extensive range of shopping options, from designer names to smaller independent stores

Souvenirs

Simple souvenirs can be found at the Magnificent Mile malls, but more choices at better prices can be found among the touristy shops of Navy Pier. Alternatives to miniatures of high-rise buildings, such as Willis Tower and Hancock Tower, and T-shirts, plates and fridge magnets bearing images of the skyline seen from Lake Michigan include the genuine municipal cast-offs, such as sewer covers and parking meters, offered by the City of Chicago Store on E. Pearson Street.

Tasty Reminders

Sausages might seem an unlikely reminder of Chicago but the city has been shaped by people of Eastern European descent, with the result that Polish handmade sausages (and those of other Eastern European nationalities), with various meats, flavorings and spices, are a feature of many delis. For a quick bite, try the distinctive hot dogs and deep-dish pizza.

Books and Music

Surviving the rising tide of international chains, Chicago retains an impressive number of independent bookstores; 57th Street in Hyde Park holds several. Likewise, the city's strong jazz and blues pedigree is represented by specialist CD and vinyl outlets often featuring new Chicago-based musicians alongside established names.

SPORTING SOUVENIRS

The city that produced basketball's Michael Jordan and made a celebrity of baseball's Sammy Sosa is unsurprisingly rich in sporting lore and offers mementoes and much memorabilia. Baseball's White Sox and Cubs both have outlets close to their stadiums, and that of the latter, the legendary Wrigley Field, has a souvenir industry all of its own. The merchandise of football's Chicago Bears and basketball's Chicago Bulls is also prevalent around the city.

Shopping by Theme

Whether you're looking for a department store, a quirky boutique or something in between, you'll find it all in Chicago. On this page shops are listed by theme. For a more detailed write-up, see the individual listings in Chicago by Area.

After sunset, much of the Magnificent Mile (▷ 68) and parts of the Loop are bathed in twinkling lights. The Wrigley Building (▷ 72) seen from Michigan Avenue Bridge is famously stunning, while the illuminated profile of the John Hancock Center (▷ 60) makes the towering building seem even taller. From it, or the Willis Tower (▷ 28–29), a nighttime viewing reveals the grid-style patterns of city neighborhoods stretching into the distance and the blackness of Lake Michigan dotted by the lights of ships.

Warm Nights

Warm nights during spring, summer and fall find Chicagoans outdoors, making the most of bars and restaurants with patio tables. With its hotels and late-opening shops, the Magnificent Mile is lively after dark, but there is more taking place in the nightlife strips of residential neighborhoods. The Gold Coast sections of Division, Oak and Elm streets are worth a look, as are the main drags of Wicker Park and Lake View. More commercially oriented nightlife is found amid the theme bars and clubs of River North. The cool breezes and live music at Navy Pier make a summertime stroll a "must."

Winter Wonders

Cold and snowy Chicago may sometimes be, but dull it never is. The winter period marks a high point of the cultural calendar with the classical concert, opera and ballet seasons fully into their stride, and a complete program of theater, rock and pop music.

There are plenty of clubs and theaters to keep visitors entertained after dark

CHICAGO BLUES

When the nationwide chain of House of Blues opened in the River North entertainment district in the 1990s, it marked a full circle for the city where South Side clubs gave birth to the urban electric blues. In such places, generally smaller and friendlier than the more tourist-oriented North Side venues, electric blues can still be heard.

ESSENTIAL CHICAGO CHICAGO BY NIGHT

13

Eating Out

Chicago is a city of hearty appetites, guaranteeing you a good meal whether at a local hot-dog stand or at a marquee restaurant. Headquarters to the nation's slaughterhouses in the 19th century, Chicago is famed for its steak houses, such as the classic Gene & Georgetti's, and beef sandwich shops. In recent years it has emerged as a culinary leader in fine dining, with celebrated meals from top chefs Charlie Trotter (Charlie Trotter's) and Rick Bayless (Frontera Grill and Topolobampo) and next-generation culinary experimenter Grant Achatz (Alinea).

Ethnic Eats

Immigrant neighborhoods of Poles, Indians, Vietnamese, Chinese and Italians, among others, lay their tables richly with authentic homeland foods; visit Milwaukee Avenue for Polish borscht, Devon Street for Indian *dal*, Argyle Street for Vietnamese *pho*, Greektown's Halsted Street for *saganaki* or Chinatown for dim sum. Tasty and often thrifty adventures with myriad dining choices line those streets.

Deep-Dish Pizza

To sample Chicago's famous deep-dish pizza requires a hearty appetite. It consists of a pie-shaped pizza crust filled with mozzarella cheese, your choice of meat and vegetables, and topped with a heaping amount of Italian-flavored tomato sauce. Unlike New York-styled pizza, which is thin and flat, a single slice of deep dish pizza can be a meal in itself.

CHICAGO-STYLE HOT DOGS

Chicago-style hot dogs are sold in hundreds of restaurants across the city. To eat one like a true Chicagoan, you must never order ketchup on it. Instead, try to find a restaurant that sells Vienna Beef brand hot dogs and order it with mustard and lots of vegetables—like chopped onions, tomatoes, a pickle and sport peppers. Eat it on a steamed poppy-seed bun and with a side order of french fries—where ketchup is allowed.

Try Chicago's famed deep-dish pizzas, or dine at a range of superb restaurants

Restaurants by Cuisine

There are restaurants to suit all tastes and budgets in Chicago. On this page they are listed by cuisine. For a more detailed description of each restaurant, see Chicago by Area.

ASIAN

Arun's (▷ 106)
Ben Pao (▷ 79)
Emperor's Choice (▷ 94)
Opera (▷ 94)
Phoenix (▷ 94)

CAJUN

Calypso Café (▷ 94)

CONTEMPORARY AMERICAN

Alinea (▷ 79)
Atwood Café (▷ 37)
Bin 36 (▷ 79)
Charlie Trotter's (▷ 79)
Exchequer (▷ 37)
Garden Restaurant (▷ 54)
Park Grill (▷ 54)
Rhapsody (▷ 38)
South Water Kitchen
  (▷ 38)
Spring (▷ 106)
Tavern at the Park (▷ 54)

ECLECTIC

Aria (▷ 54)
Grand Lux Café (▷ 80)
Seven on State (▷ 38)

EAST EUROPEAN

Barbakan Restaurant
  (▷ 106)
Café Lura (▷ 106)
Russian Tea Time (▷ 38)

FRENCH

Bistro 110 (▷ 79)
Bistro Campagne (▷ 106)
Brasserie Jo (▷ 79)
Everest (▷ 37)
La Petite Folie (▷ 94)

GERMAN

The Berghoff (▷ 37)
Chicago Brauhaus (▷ 106)

ITALIAN

312 Chicago (▷ 37)
Club Lucky (▷ 106)
Gino's East (▷ panel 80)
Gioco (▷ 94)
Giordano's (▷ panel 80)
The Italian Village
  Restaurants (▷ 37)
Maggiano's Little Italy
  (▷ 80)
Mia Francesca (▷ 106)
Petterino's (▷ 38)
Pizzeria Uno (▷ panel 80)
Rosebud on Rush (▷ 80)
Trattoria No. 10 (▷ 38)

MEXICAN

Adobo Grill (▷ 79)
Frontera Grill/
  Topolobampo (▷ 80)
Zapatista (▷ 94)

QUICK BITES

Big Bowl Café (▷ 79)
Corner Bakery Café
  (▷ 54)
Ed Debevic's Short Order
  Deluxe (▷ 79)
Lou Mitchell's (▷ 38)
Potbelly Sandwich Works
  (▷ 38)

SEAFOOD

Riva (▷ 80)
Soundings Café (▷ 54)

STEAKS, RIBS, CHOPS

Custom House (▷ 37)
Gene & Georgetti (▷ 80)
Morton's of Chicago
  (▷ 80)
Nine (▷ 38)
The Palm (▷ 54)
Ruth's Chris Steakhouse
  (▷ 38)

If You Like...

However you'd like to spend your time in Chicago, these top suggestions should help you tailor your ideal visit. Each suggestion has a fuller write-up elsewhere in the book.

CARTING THE KIDS

See the dolphin show at the John G. Shedd Aquarium (▷ 49).
Hit Navy Pier (▷ 64) for the Children's Museum and Ferris wheel.
Make the acquantaince of T. rex Sue at the Field Museum (▷ 46).
Visit the apes at the Lincoln Park Zoo (▷ 62).

OGLING THE ARCHITECTURE

Trek to Frank Lloyd Wright's Home and Studio (▷ 100).
Take the Architecture River Cruise with the Chicago Architecture Foundation (▷ 24).
Tour the Robie House (▷ 91).
Visit the Glessner House (▷ 87).

The fun of the fair at Navy Pier; dining out; go see a show or visit a comedy club

SAVING MONEY

Dine on Chicago hot dogs or personal deep-dish pizzas.
Ride the El for a budget skyline tour (▷ 26).
Go to the Lincoln Park Zoo (▷ 62); it's free.
Catch a band outdoors at the Navy Pier beer garden, also free (▷ 64).

SHOW GOING

Get tickets to the Goodman Theatre (▷ 36) in the Loop.
Spot the celebs on stage at the Steppenwolf Theater (▷ 77).
Laugh it up at Second City (▷ 67).

DINING WITH A VIEW

Reserve a table at Everest (▷ 37) for western views.

Dine amid the skyline at the Signature Room on the 95th floor in the John Hancock Building (▷ 60).

Go to NoMI, which frames the Historic Water Tower (▷ 112, Park Hyatt Chicago) from its seventh-floor perch.

Regard the Lake Michigan views from this waterfront location at Riva (▷ 80).

NIGHTCRAWLING

Hit the Green Mill Cocktail Lounge (▷ 104) for a live jazz set.

Get the blues at Buddy Guy's Legends (▷ 35).

Check out the local and touring acts on stage at the Metro (▷ 104).

Visit Stone Lotus (▷ 77) and soak up the scene.

Enjoy fine dining, live music clubs and shopping for Cubs items or cutting-edge fashion

SOUVENIR SHOPPING

Illinois Artisans Shop (▷ 33) for local artist-made crafts.

Navy Pier shops for trinkets, snowglobes and Chicago Police Department T-shirts (▷ 75).

City of Chicago Store for street signs and even parking meters.

Hit the Wrigley Field (▷ 59) region for Cubs paraphernalia.

FASHION WITH EDGE

Ultimo (▷ 75) for a mix of high-end designers.

City Soles (▷ 99) for funky shoes.

P45 (▷ 99) for emerging American designers.

GOING GREEN

Walk the art- and architecture-filled
Millennium Park (▷ 50).
Get to Grant Park (▷ 51) in the evening
for a look at Buckingham Fountain's
light show.
Visit the greenhouses of the
Garfield Park Conservatory
(▷ 102).
Tour Lincoln Park, home to a zoo,
conservatory, gardens and beaches
(▷ 62, 71).

OUTWARD-BOUND ACTION

Ride a bike along 18 miles
(29km) of shoreline parkway
(▷ 84).
**Get in on a game of sand
volleyball** at the North Avenue
Beach (▷ 66).
Swim with the triathletes in Lake Michigan.

LOCAL FOOD

Have a hot dog filled with vegetables at Gold
Coast Dogs (▷ panel, 79).
Line up for a high-fat breakfast at Lou
Mitchell's (▷ 38).
Devour a slice or two of deep-dish pizza at
Gino's East or Pizzeria Uno (▷ panel, 80).
Tuck into Italian classic dishes at Rosebud on
Rush or Maggiano's Little Italy (▷ 80).

*Burn off the calories then
indulge on pizza or take
tea at the Ritz-Carlton*

HAUT HOTELS

Have high tea at the Ritz-Carlton Chicago
(▷ 112).
Be pampered at the spa in the
Peninsula hotel (▷ panel, 112).
Admire the sparkling city lights from
the Trump International Hotel and Tower
or its Rebar cocktail lounge (▷ 112).
Ogle the multimillion-dollar art collection
at the Park Hyatt Chicago (▷ 112).

The Loop

Named for the elevated train that rings the district, the downtown Loop is where Chicago does business. The historic center is also the seat of government and the oldest shopping district in the city.

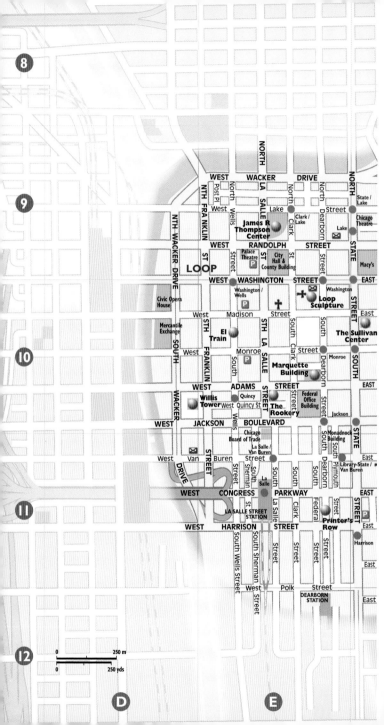

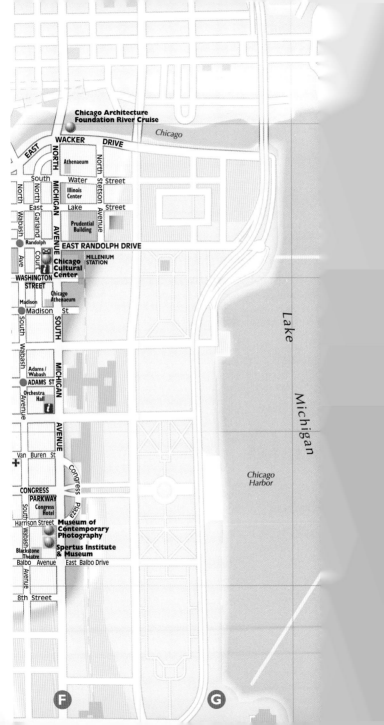

Chicago Architecture Foundation River Cruise

Chicago cruise boats

THE BASICS

www.architecture.org

🔲 F9

✉ 224 Michigan Avenue (board at dock location at Michigan Avenue and Wacker Drive)

☎ 312/922-3432

🕐 10 sailings daily in summer. Closed Dec–Apr

Ⓜ Brown Line: Randolph

🚌 144, 146, 151

✋ Expensive

HIGHLIGHTS

● Wrigley Building
● Marina Towers
● 333 W. Wacker Drive
● Chicago River bridges
● Willis Tower
● Tribune Tower

The best of the boat cruises that ply the Chicago River, the Chicago Architecture Foundation's river tours provide knowledgeable narration of 50 distinctive buildings in popular 90-minute outings.

Architectural historians Founded by architects and preservationists in 1966 to preserve the Glessner House on Prairie Avenue, the Chicago Architecture Foundation has grown into the city's most respected leader of design-oriented tours. Arresting buildings loom over passengers gliding by at their bases at water level. Volunteer docents (guides) narrate the trip, covering Bertrand Goldberg's 1964 corn-cob-shape Marina City Towers, the triangular, white, tile-clad Wrigley Building erected by the chewing-gum magnate William Wrigley Jr., the black granite art deco tower of the Carbide & Carbon Building from the sons of city planner Daniel Burnham and the 1922-erected Tribune Building that, crowned by a series of Gothic flying buttresses inspired by a French cathedral, looks much older. New city landmarks include the shiny Trump Hotel and the Aqua building.

Chicago River In the 17th century Native Americans occupied the banks of the Chicago River where it met Lake Michigan. Over the next centuries as the population grew, wastewater from the river flowed into Lake Michigan, contaminating the city's drinking water. So in 1900 engineers reversed the river's flow away from the lake and into the Sanitary and Ship Canal.

Loop Public Sculpture

A few blocks in Chicago's Loop district comprise an outdoor exhibition space devoted to some of the world's finest sculptors. It's ideal for those looking for a cultural self-guided walking tour.

The collection In 1967 then-mayor Richard J. Daley dedicated the monumental, untitled sculpture by Pablo Picasso at Daley Center Plaza (Dearborn and Washington streets), considered the first noncommemorative city sculpture and the start of Chicago's strong public arts program highlighted by its collection in the Loop. Across Washington Street, Joan Miró's depiction of a woman with outstretched arms faces the Picasso. Marc Chagall's stone mosaic *The Four Seasons* is at Dearborn and Monroe streets. Two blocks down at Dearborn and Adams, Alexander Calder's graceful, neon orange *Flamingo* contrasts with the dark glass Federal Center. Jean Dubuffet's white fiberglass *Monument with Standing Beast* resides at the James R. Thompson Center where Clark meets Randolph Street. And just over the Chicago River in the West Loop at 600 W. Madison Claes Oldenburg created *Batcolumn*, a 100ft (328m) steel baseball bat.

Chicago's Picasso Chicago architect William Hartman convinced Pablo Picasso to create a sculpture for the city's Civic Center Plaza. Picasso's untitled work, "a gift to the people of Chicago," is today part of everyday Loop life, and skateboarders launch from its sloping base.

THE BASICS

www.cityofchicago.org/
publicart

✚ E10

Ⓘ Brown, Red, Green
Loop stops

🚌 20, 22

HIGHLIGHTS

● *Untitled* by Pablo Picasso
● *Flamingo* by Alexander Calder
● *Monument with Standing Beast* by Jean Dubuffet
● *Chicago* by Joan Miró
● *Batcolumn* by Claus Oldenburg
● *The Four Seasons* by Marc Chagall

THE LOOP

TOP 25

Riding the El Train

The El Train crossing the Chicago River (left); Quincy station (right)

THE BASICS

www.transitchicago.com

🚉 E10

☎ 888/968-7282

🕐 Mon–Sat 5am–1am, Sun 7.16am–12.17am

🚇 Brown Line Loop stops

🚌 29

🖐 Inexpensive

HIGHLIGHTS

● Crossing the Chicago River aboard the Brown Line
● Seeing into baseball's Wrigley Field from the Addison stop on the Red Line
● Snaking around the downtown high-rises aboard the Brown Line

FACTS

● Blue Line, largely underground, efficiently connects O'Hare airport to downtown.
● The elevated Orange Line links Midway Airport and downtown.

One of Chicago's most distinctive symbols, the elevated train, El or L for short, provides a commuter's close-up of the city's downtown district as well as its neighborhood backyards.

Tracking history New York erected the first elevated train in 1867, a feat Chicago soon copied, with a flurry of companies devoted to the project. The first line (3.6 miles/5.8km) opened in 1892 and was nicknamed the "Alley L" for running above city-owned alleys, sparing the transit company from securing access privileges from the property owners. Expansion of the El lines was linked to many major events in Chicago history including the World's Columbian Exhibition and the need to get workers to the Stock Yards. Independently owned rail lines agreed to link their services downtown in a "Union Loop" in 1897, the origin of the district's name. Chicago Transit Authority today operates eight color-coded routes over 242 miles (389km) of track.

Brown Line The best line for sightseers, the Brown Line rings the downtown Loop, crosses the Chicago River heading north through the neighborhoods of River North, Lincoln Park, Lakeview and Lincoln Square before terminating at Kimball Street. Board anywhere in the Loop to enjoy weaving through the high-rises two stories up from street level. Disembark at any stop on the route and, using overhead platform bridges that connect north- and southbound tracks without a transfer fee, return in the opposite direction.

The Rookery

Interior of The Rookery building (left); detail of the exterior of the building (right)

Designed by Daniel Burnham and John Wellborn Root in the 1880s, and later renovated by Frank Lloyd Wright, the Rookery is among Chicago's most admired landmarks.

Birdhouse After the Great Fire of 1871, birds took to roosting in the water-storage building that was temporarily City Hall. It was consequently nicknamed the Rookery. Public feeling dictated that the building that replaced it should formally take on this name. Rising 11 floors, the Rookery was among the tallest buildings in the world on completion and one of the most important early skyscrapers. The thick load-bearing brick-and-granite walls at the base, decorated with Roman, Moorish and Venetian (and several rook) motifs, support upper levels with an iron frame that enabled the structure to be raised higher than previously thought possible. With its masonry exterior and iron interior, the Rookery is considered by architectural historians to be a transitional building in the evolution of the modern skyscraper.

Interior treasures The facade, however, is scant preparation for the interior. The inner court is bathed in incredible levels of natural light entering through a vast domed skylight. Imposing lamps hang above the floor, and Root's intricate ironwork decorates the stairways that climb up to a 360-degree balcony. The white marble, introduced by Frank Lloyd Wright in 1905, increases the sense of space and brightness.

THE BASICS

www.therookerybuilding.com
+ E10
⊠ 209 S. La Salle Street
☎ 312/553-6100
◷ Lobby open during business hours
Ⓡ Brown and Orange Lines: Quincy
🚌 1, 22, 60, 151
♿ Good
🎟 Free

HIGHLIGHTS

● Light-flooded, glass-roofed inner court
● Ten-story spiral staircase
● Prairie-style light fixtures
● External terra-cotta ornamentation
● Carrara marble walls
● Mosaic tile floors

Willis Tower

HIGHLIGHTS

- Visibility of up to 50 miles (80km) on a clear day
- Standing on The Ledge and daring to look down
- Feeling the building sway
- High-powered telescopes
- Sunset views after 4pm
- Terminals with tower information in several languages

FACTS

- Six robotic window washers mounted on the roof clean all the 16,000 windows.
- Elevators soar 1,600ft (487m) per minute.

Formerly known as the Sears Tower, the Willis Tower rises higher than any other structure in the city. As well as stylish architecture, it has the highest man-made vantage point in the western hemisphere and the vertigo-inducing Ledge.

Built from tubes From 1974 to 1996, the Willis Tower's 110 floors and 1,454ft (443m) height made it the tallest building in the world, rising from the Loop with a distinctive profile of black aluminum and bronze-tinted glass. Architect Bruce Graham, of Skidmore, Owings & Merrill, structured it around nine 75sq ft (7sq m) bundled tubes, which decline in number as the building reaches upward. Aside from increasing the colossal structure's strength, this technique also echoes the stepback, New York skyscraper style of the late

Clockwise from top left: People on the observation deck of the Willis Tower; the Chicago skyline seen from the Willis Tower; looking down to the Chicago River from the tower; the most amazing view from The Ledge

1920s. Among the early tasks during the three-year construction was the creation of foundation supports capable of holding a 222,500-ton building. The two rooftop antennae were added in 1982, increasing the building's height by 253ft (77m). Sears, the retail company that commissioned the building of the tower and used its lower floors, moved out in 1992.

Seeing for miles The 103rd-floor Skydeck is accessible via a 70-second elevator ride, and reveals an invigorating panorama of the city and its surroundings. An interesting recorded commentary describes the view and landmark buildings. Step out onto The Ledge, a glass-bottomed window extension that lets you look straight down to the city streets and river 1,354ft (412m) below—not recommended if you have a fear of heights.

THE BASICS

www.theskydeck.com

D10

233 S. Wacker Drive

312/875-9696

Skydeck: Apr–Sep daily 9am–10pm; Oct–Mar daily 10–8. May be closed in high winds

Various restaurants and cafés

Brown and Orange Lines: Quincy

1, 60, 151, 156

Excellent

Moderate

More to See

CHICAGO CULTURAL CENTER

www.chicagoculturalcenter.org

The Washington Street entrance leads through hefty bronze doors beneath a Romanesque portal into the lobby, whose grand staircase is bordered by exquisite mosaics set into white Carrara marble balustrades. The second floor has the hall and rotunda of the Great Army of the Republic, with Tennessee marble walls and mosaic tile floor, while the floor above holds the Preston Bradley Hall, with an awe-inspiring Tiffany-glass dome. The main exhibition hall on the top level features columns that rise to meet a coffered ceiling. The Randolph Street entrance leads to a visitor information center and café.

➕ F9 ✉ 78 E. Washington Street ☎ 312/744-6630 🕐 Mon–Thu 8–7, Fri 8–6, Sat 9–6, Sun 10–6 🍽 Café 🚇 Brown and Orange Lines: Madison 🚌 3, 4, 60, 145, 147, 151

JAMES R. THOMPSON CENTER

www.cms.il.gov

This distinctive glass-and-steel edifice includes a soaring atrium that is lined with stores, restaurants and cafés; the upper levels house state agencies.

➕ E9 ✉ 100 W. Randolph Street ☎ 312/814-6684 🚇 Blue, Brown and Orange Lines: Clark/Lake 🚌 156 ♿ Good

MARQUETTE BUILDING

Completed in 1895, this building is among the unsung masterpieces of Chicago architecture. It demonstrates the first use of the three-part "Chicago window"—plate glass spans the whole width between the building's steel supports. Lobby reliefs record the expedition of French Jesuit missionary Jacques Marquette; the entrance doors' panther heads are by Edward Kemeys, also responsible for the lions fronting the Art Institute of Chicago (▷ 44).

➕ E10 ✉ 140 S. Dearborn Street 🚇 Brown and Orange Lines: Quincy

MUSEUM OF CONTEMPORARY PHOTOGRAPHY

www.mocp.org

In addition to the collection of American photography, varied temporary exhibitions feature contemporary photography from around the world.

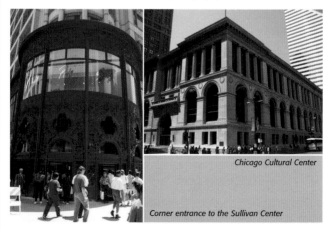

Chicago Cultural Center

Corner entrance to the Sullivan Center

F11 ✉ 600 S. Michigan Avenue ☎ 312/663-5554 🕐 Mon–Sat 10–5 (Thu till 8), Sun 12–5 🚇 Red Line: Harrison 🚌 1, 3, 4, 6, 38, 146 ♿ Good ✋ Free

F11 ✉ 610 S. Michigan Avenue ☎ 312/322-1700 🕐 Museum second Thu of month 5.30–8, alternate Sun 10.30–3 🚇 Red Line: Harrison 🚌 1, 3, 4, 6, 38, 146 ♿ Good ✋ Moderate

PRINTER'S ROW

The industrial buildings lining Dearborn Street were the core of Chicago's printing industry during the late 19th century. Many are now loft-style apartments, with galleries and restaurants.
E11 ✉ Dearborn Street 🚇 Blue line: La Salle; Red Line: Harrison 🚌 22, 62

SPERTUS INSTITUTE & MUSEUM

www.spertus.edu

Torah scrolls, Hanukkah menorahs and circumcision tools are among the decorative and religious objects spanning 5,000 years featured in the museum's collection of Judaica. The richness of most exhibits contrasts strongly with the somber collection of Holocaust memorabilia. Its new building, which opened in November 2007, added a kosher café run by chef Wolfgang Puck, a children's center, an expanded gift shop and a 400-seat theater.

THE SULLIVAN CENTER

The elaborately decorated exterior of the former Carson Pirie Scott building was created by Louis Sullivan over a five-year period beginning in 1899. The more austere terra-cotta-clad upper levels express the steel form of the building. The large windows span the entire width between steel supports: known as "Chicago windows," they accentuate the horizontal, maximize the amount of natural light reaching the interior and strengthen the general sense of geometric cohesion. A 2001–09 renovation restored many of Sullivan's features and the building was redeveloped as The Sullivan Center, housing retail and office space and The School of the Art Institute of Chicago.
F10 ✉ 1 S. State Street 🚇 Blue line: Madison; Red Line: Monroe 🚌 22, 23, 36, 56, 157 ♿ Good ✋ Free

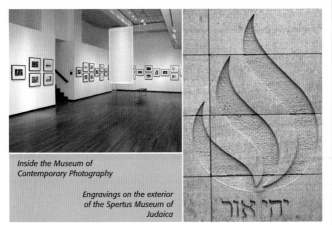

Inside the Museum of Contemporary Photography

Engravings on the exterior of the Spertus Museum of Judaica

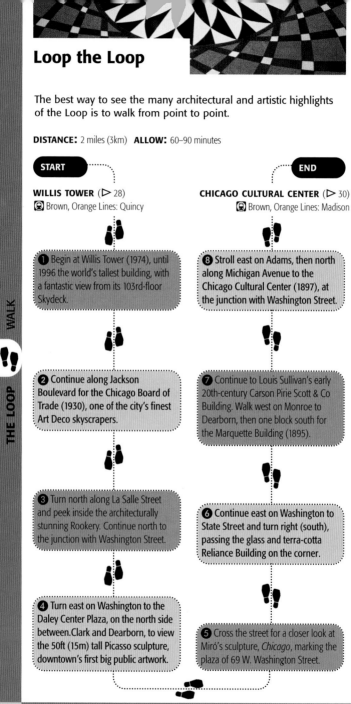

Loop the Loop

The best way to see the many architectural and artistic highlights of the Loop is to walk from point to point.

DISTANCE: 2 miles (3km) **ALLOW:** 60–90 minutes

START

WILLIS TOWER (▷ 28)
🚇 Brown, Orange Lines: Quincy

END

CHICAGO CULTURAL CENTER (▷ 30)
🚇 Brown, Orange Lines: Madison

1 Begin at Willis Tower (1974), until 1996 the world's tallest building, with a fantastic view from its 103rd-floor Skydeck.

8 Stroll east on Adams, then north along Michigan Avenue to the Chicago Cultural Center (1897), at the junction with Washington Street.

2 Continue along Jackson Boulevard for the Chicago Board of Trade (1930), one of the city's finest Art Deco skyscrapers.

7 Continue to Louis Sullivan's early 20th-century Carson Pirie Scott & Co Building. Walk west on Monroe to Dearborn, then one block south for the Marquette Building (1895).

3 Turn north along La Salle Street and peek inside the architecturally stunning Rookery. Continue north to the junction with Washington Street.

6 Continue east on Washington to State Street and turn right (south), passing the glass and terra-cotta Reliance Building on the corner.

4 Turn east on Washington to the Daley Center Plaza, on the north side between.Clark and Dearborn, to view the 50ft (15m) tall Picasso sculpture, downtown's first big public artwork.

5 Cross the street for a closer look at Miró's sculpture, *Chicago*, marking the plaza of 69 W. Washington Street.

WALK

THE LOOP

Shopping

ARTS & ARTISANS
www.artsartisans.com
For beautiful, one-of-a-kind gifts, visit this family-run store selling fine American crafts, art and jewelry; everything from glass and ceramics to metal sculptures and wood carvings. They can even help you arrange custom-designed pieces.
🚇 F9 ✉ 35 E. Wacker Drive ☎ 312/578-0126 🚇 Brown, Green, Orange, Pink, Purple Lines: State/Lake 🚌 29, 143, 144, 145, 146, 151

THE ATRIUM MALL
Diverse stores provide an excellent excuse to take a look around the spectacular second floor of this dazzling atrium, a pastiche of glass, marble and steel, with an impressive waterfall.
🚇 E9 ✉ James R. Thompson Center, 100 W. Randolph Street ☎ 312/346-0777 🚇 Blue, Brown, Orange Lines: Clark/Lake 🚌 156

BLICK ART MATERIALS
Art supply store Blick stocks everything from oil paints to sculptor's clay. Sketchpads and kids' projects may appeal to travelers.
🚇 F10 ✉ 42 S. State Street ☎ 312/920-0300 🚇 Red Line: Madison 🚌 29

BOOKSAMILLION
There could well be over a million books, mostly mainstream titles on diverse subjects, amid these tightly stacked shelves.
🚇 E10 ✉ 144 S. Clark Street ☎ 312/857-0613 🚇 Blue, Red Lines: Washington 🚌 22, 24

CHICAGO ARCHITECTURE FOUNDATION
www.architecture.org
Exemplary source of books on architecture, as well as clever, colorful gifts that make tasteful souvenirs.
🚇 F11 ✉ 224 S. Michigan Avenue ☎ 312/922-3432 🚇 Brown, Orange Lines: Adams 🚌 3, 4, 6, 38

GRAHAM CRACKERS COMICS
www.grahamcrackers.com
This well-stocked comic-book store appeals to the area's college students and comic aficionados.
🚇 F10 ✉ 77 E. Madison Street ☎ 312/629-1810 🚇 Red Line: Madison 🚌 29

PRINTER'S ROW BOOK FAIR
To celebrate the district's history in print production the annual Printer's Row Book Fair, held over a weekend in early June, lures new, used and antiques booksellers to temporary shops under tents lining South Dearborn between Congress and Polk. Event programs include author readings and signings, and discussions.

H&M
This Swedish designer knock-off shop, with featured lines by some actual designers including Stella McCartney, sells cheap and chic women's clothing.
🚇 F9 ✉ 20 N. State Street ☎ 312/263-4436 🚇 Red Line: Washington 🚌 29

ILLINOIS ARTISANS SHOP
On the second floor of the James R. Thompson Center, Illinois Artisans Shop showcases the work of artists around the state working in jewelry, ceramics, wood and textiles with semiannual exhibits of fine art, including painting, photography, printmaking, drawing and sculpture.
🚇 E9 ✉ James R. Thompson Center, 100 W. Randolph Street ☎ 312/814-5321 🚇 Blue, Brown, Orange Lines: Clark/Lake 🚌 156

THE JEWELER'S CENTER
www.jewelerscenter.com
Jewelry and related products are sold in more than 190 outlets over 13 floors; if you can't find what you're looking for here, you never will.
🚇 F10 ✉ 5 S. Wabash Avenue ☎ 312/424-2664 🚇 Brown, Orange Lines: Madison 🚌 38

LOEHMANN'S
www.loehmanns.com
Whether you're looking for casual fashions or

more conservative business attire, you'll find two spacious floors of top brand names and designer labels at significantly discounted prices, plus shoes and accessories.
➕ F10 ✉ 151 N. State Street ☎ 312/705-3810 🚇 Blue, Red Lines: Washington 🚌 6, 11, 29, 36, 44, 62, 146

MACY'S
www.visitmacyschicago.com
Once home to the beloved Marshall Fields department store, the New York-based Macy's chain took over in 2006, much to the disgust of many Chicagoans. But Macy's retained many of the old store's famous features, including decorated windows at Christmas and the ornate, century-old green clock that hangs outside. Inside, the store sells clothing, home goods, food items and jewelry. It also houses several restaurants, such as the legendary Walnut Room, and many unique "stores within a store." The Frango Mint candies make a nice Chicago souvenir.
➕ F10 ✉ 111 N. State Street ☎ 312/781-1000 🚇 Blue, Red Lines: Washington 🚌 6, 11, 29, 36, 44, 62, 146

NORDSTROM RACK
www.nordstrom.com
The Rack takes up to 70 percent off full-price goods sold at sibling retailer Nordstrom, a Seattle-based department store best known for its quality clothing and shoe selection.
➕ F10 ✉ 24 N. State Street ☎ 312/377-5500 🚇 Red Line: Washington 🚌 29

OLD NAVY
www.oldnavy.com
A lower-cost spin-off from the popular casual clothier Gap, Old Navy dresses infants to seniors in inexpensive, on-trend styles that make no pretense to endure more than a season. Shop to a disco soundtrack on two levels.
➕ F10 ✉ 35 N. State Street ☎ 312/551-0522 🚇 Red Line: Washington 🚌 29

POSTER PLUS
www.posterplus.com
Historic posters, mostly celebrating landmarks in Chicago and US history, though many are attractive reprints

GARRETT POPCORN
People line up for blocks to buy their Caramelcrisp, Cheesecorn and butter versions of this popcorn, which is popular with tourists and celebrities. Mix a few of your favorite types together in a bag, box or decorative tin. They have four Loop locations: 26 W. Randolph, 2 W. Jackson, 4 E. Madison, and 500 W. Madison (Citicorp Center). To find out more visit their website at www.garrettpopcorn.com.

rather than originals.
➕ F11 ✉ 200 S. Michigan Avenue ☎ 312/461-9277 🚇 Brown, Orange Lines: Adams 🚌 3, 4, 6, 38

POWELL'S BOOKSTORE
www.powellschicago.com
New, used and discount bookstore primarily serving local universities, with a strong collection of classics.
➕ F12 ✉ 828 S. Wabash Avenue ☎ 312/341-0748 🚇 Red Line: Harrison 🚌 129

SYD JEROME
www.sydjerome.com
Esquire magazine rated this upscale men's store "Best in Class" for its impeccably stylish and elegant fashions coming from the likes of Armani, Hickey Freeman and Jhane Barnes.
➕ E10 ✉ 2 N. LaSalle Street ☎ 312/346 0333 🚇 Brown, Orange, Pink, Purple Lines: Washington/ Wells 🚌 134, 135, 136, 156

T. J. MAXX
www.tjmaxx.com
Another discount clothing chain; this one assembles mid-market looks for women.
➕ F9 ✉ 11 N. State Street ☎ 312/553-0515 🚇 Red Line: Washington 🚌 29

Entertainment and Nightlife

AUDITORIUM THEATRE
www.auditoriumtheatre.org
Designed by the revered Adler & Sullivan, the marvelously renovated Auditorium Building was the world's heaviest structure when completed in 1889. Excellent acoustics and good sightlines make it a fine venue for dance, music and drama productions.
F11 ⊠ 50 E. Congress Parkway ☎ 312/922-2110
Red Line: Harrison
6, 145, 146, 147, 151

BANK OF AMERICA THEATER
Dating back to the 19th century, this handsome place is a rare reminder that theater once thrived in the Loop. Dance companies perform here, though it is not exclusively a dance theater. It is best known for its musicals.
F10 ⊠ 18 W. Monroe Street ☎ 312/977-1701
Brown, Orange Lines: Madison/Wells 29

BASE BAR
www.hardrockhotelchicago.com
The trendy lobby bar in the Hard Rock Hotel rocks out via a ministage that hosts live impromptu shows, sometimes by major stars, and TVs showing music videos.
F9 ⊠ 230 N. Michigan Avenue ☎ 312/345-1000
Red Line: Lake 143, 144, 145, 146

BIG BAR
www.chicagoregency.hyatt.com
Size is everything at this boisterous bar in the Hyatt Regency Chicago, credited with making the world's largest margarita, in a cement mixer.
F9 ⊠ 151 E. Wacker Drive ☎ 312/565-1234
Red Line: Lake 143, 144, 145, 146

BUDDY GUY'S LEGENDS
www.buddyguys.com
Co-owner and famed blues guitarist Buddy Guy presents outstanding blues acts, including internationally known names and local rising stars.
F11 ⊠ 754 S. Wabash Avenue ☎ 312/427-1190
Red Line: Harrison 12

CADILLAC PALACE THEATRE
www.broadwayinchicago.com
One of the major theaters

COMEDY SHOWS

Two comedy shows have been entertaining Chicago theatergoers for years. *Tony 'n' Tina's Wedding* (⊠ 230 W. North Avenue ☎ 312/664-8844) re-creates an Italian-American wedding; the performers mingle with the audience (the guests). While, *Late Nite Catechism* (⊠ Royal George Theater, 1641 N. Halsted ☎ 312/988-9000) is a hilarious, interactive one-woman show on Thursday and Saturday.

---

along Randolph Street, comprising the Loop's theater district, the Cadillac Palace is often booked by big Broadway touring companies.
E9 ⊠ 151 W. Randolph Street ☎ 312/977-1700
Brown, Orange Lines: Washington 156

CHASE AUDITORIUM
www.npr.org
The satirical National Public Radio news-quiz show "Wait, Wait…Don't Tell me!" tapes its shows live most Thursday nights in this bank building basement auditorium.
E10 ⊠ 10 S. Dearborn Street ☎ 888/924-8924
Red Line: Monroe
29

CHICAGO THEATRE
www.thechicagotheatre.com
The 3,600-seat, French baroque-style Chicago Theatre, with the classic vertical C-H-I-C-A-G-O spelled out on the marquee, hosts concert tours in rock, jazz, hip-hop and ballet, as well as limited-run theater productions.
F9 ⊠ 175 N. State Street ☎ 312/462-6300 Red Line: Lake 29

CIVIC OPERA HOUSE
www.civicoperahouse.com
The fine Lyric Opera of Chicago company perform from late September to the end of March at this art deco auditorium (which is also one of the main dance venues). Seats are sometimes

available at the box office on the day of the performance.
🚇 D10 ✉ 20 N. Wacker Drive ☎ 312/419-0033 Ⓜ Brown, Orange Lines: Madison/Wells 🚌 129

ENCORE LIQUID LOUNGE
www.encorechicago.com
Run by the adjacent Hotel Allegro, next to the Cadillac Palace Theatre, Encore is a popular spot to gather for drinks before or after the curtain. A substantial list of small-plate appetizers such as chili-orange duck quesadillas with mango salsa complements the cocktails.
🚇 E9 ✉ 171 W. Randolph Street ☎ 312/338-3788 Ⓜ Brown Line: Washington 🚌 156

FORD CENTER FOR THE PERFORMING ARTS/ ORIENTAL THEATER
Still called the Oriental by locals, this ornate, 2,180-seat theater reopened in 1998 after a painstaking restoration. The North Loop theater presents first-rate shows in its top-notch performance space.
🚇 E9 ✉ 24 W. Randolph Street ☎ 312/902-1400 Ⓜ Red, Brown, Green, Orange Lines: Lake 🚌 156

GENE SISKEL FILM CENTER
www..siskelfilmcenter.org
The School of the Arts

Institute of Chicago runs this ambitious cinema named for a former, highly influential film critic. Two screens show independent, foreign and vintage films in repertory, the type of arty fare you won't find at the normal Cineplex.
🚇 F9 ✉ 164 N. State Street ☎ 312/846-2600 Ⓜ Red Line: Lake 🚌 29

GOODMAN THEATRE
www.goodmantheatre.org
The Goodman hosts some of the best drama in the city, including both classics and cutting-edge contemporary productions. Well-known actors including Brian Dehenny and Marcia Gay Harden have performed here and playwrights August Wilson and Arthur Miller debuted plays here.
🚇 E9 ✉ 170 N. Dearborn Street ☎ 312/443-3800 Ⓜ Red Line: Washington 🚌 22, 24, 36, 62

HALF-PRICE TICKETS
Hot Tix (✉ 72 E. Randolph Street or Water Works Visitor Center, 163 E. Pearson Street) offers half-price tickets for many of the day's theater events. A website (www.hottix.org) lists the day's performances. Full-price advance tickets are also available from Hot Tix, as well as from Ticketmaster (☎ 312/559-1212).

THE LIVING ROOM
www.whotels.com
The style-focused W. Chicago City Center makes a lounge of its historic lobby, installing a DJ on the mezzanine who pumps the vibe to patrons arrayed on sofas.
🚇 E10 ✉ 172 W. Adams Street ☎ 312/332-1200 Ⓜ Brown Line: Quincy 🚌 156

REDHEAD PIANO BAR
www.theredheadpianobar.com
Sit back and listen, or step up near the piano to join other patrons as they sing along to tunes ranging from "Sweet Caroline" to a Jerry Lee Lewis medley. The walls are lined with sheet music and photos of stars of yesteryear.
🚇 E8 ✉ 16 W. Ontario ☎ 312/640-1000 Ⓜ Red Line: Grand 🚌 125, 65

SYMPHONY CENTER
www.cso.org
From September to May the renowned Chicago Symphony Orchestra (CSO) is in residence in this sumptuous Greek Revival hall, built in 1904. Tickets are sold early, but some may be available on the day of performance. The Civic Orchestra of Chicago, a training orchestra, gives free concerts and there is an annual jazz series here.
🚇 F10 ✉ 220 S. Michigan Avenue ☎ 312/294-3000 Ⓜ Brown, Orange Lines: Adams 🚌 1, 3, 4, 6, 7, 38, 60

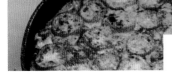

Restaurants

312 CHICAGO ($$$)

www.312chicago.com
One of the best Italian specialists in the Loop, 312 Chicago adjoins the Allegro Hotel and, like others near the theater district, requires a reservation for a table prior to showtime.

E9 136 N. La Salle Street 312/696-2420 Brown, Orange Lines: Washington 129

ATWOOD CAFÉ ($$)

www.atwoodcafe.com
Dine on hearty foods with an American accent such as maple-cured pork chops and chicken pot pie. Café staples including salads and soups lighten up the lunch fare at this window-wrapped restaurant, which views the hustle and bustle of the Loop.

E9 1 W. Washington Street 312/368-1900 Red Line: Washington 29

THE BERGHOFF ($$)

A direct descendant of one of Chicago's most fondly remembered restaurants, the historic Berghoff serves classic German fare such as *sauerbraten* and *Wiener schnitzel* in an Old World-inspired room with stained-glass accents. The café makes a great stop for lunchtime sandwiches.

E10 17 W. Adams Street 312/427-3170 Red Line: Jackson 29

CUSTOM HOUSE ($$$)

www.customhouse.cc
One of Chicago's most innovative chefs, Shawn McClain, gives the classic Chicago meat-centric menu an update with dishes such as veal cheeks and braised rabbit along with bone-in rib-eye steaks. Sleek and stylish interiors generate a clubby but unfussy vibe.

E11 Hotel Blake, 500 S. Dearborn Street 312/523-0200 Red Line: Harrison 129

DIM SUM

Served by many Chinese restaurants at lunchtime, dim sum is the term for small dishes wheeled around on trolleys. Stop a server who has dishes that look appetizing and take your pick. Popular dishes include *cha sil bow*—steamed pork bun; *gai bow*—steamed chicken bun; *chern goon*—spring rolls; and *sil mi*—steamed pork and shrimp dumpling. When you've eaten your fill, you will be charged by the plate.

EVEREST ($$$$)

www.everestrestaurant.com
This 40th-floor restaurant that commands great views—beloved of financial wheeler-dealers—offers an updated and sometimes inspiring look at chef Jean Joho's native Alsace. The Loop location, prices and standards of cooking are all breathtakingly high.

E10 440 S. La Salle Street 312/663-8920 Dinner only; closed Sun, Mon Blue Line: La Salle 22

EXCHEQUER ($$)

www.exchequerpub.com
Friendly family-run place that's always bustling thanks to its good-value ribs, pizza and classic American dishes, with some surprises like the Bistro Burger. Lots of good draught beers too.

F10 226 S. Wabash Avenue 312/939-5633 Brown, Green, Orange, Pink, Purple Lines: Adams/Wabash 7, 126, 151

THE ITALIAN VILLAGE RESTAURANTS ($$–$$$$)

www.italianvillage-chicago.com
Three Italians in one building, including the expensive and smart Vivere, the mid-priced and seafood-focused La Cantina and the affordable Village.

E10 71 W. Monroe Street 312/332-7005 Red Line: Monroe 29

LOU MITCHELL'S ($)

www.loumitchellsrestaurant.com
Longstanding Chicago diner serves fluffy omelets and homebaked pastries for which locals regularly stand in line.
✚ E9 ✉ 565 W. Jackson Boulevard ☎ 312/939-3111
⏰ Breakfast and lunch only ⓜ Brown, Orange Lines: Quincy 🚌 126

NINE ($$$$)

www.n9ne.com
Stylish steak house serving massive steaks, as well as indulgences such as caviar and tartare.
✚ E10 ✉ 440 W. Randolph Street ☎ 312/575-9900
⏰ Closed Sun ⓜ Brown Line: Washington 🚌 156

PETTERINO'S ($$$)

www.petterinos.com
Supper-club style restaurant that specializes in steaks and seafood. Adjacent to the Goodman Theatre, this is a popular pre-curtain stop.
✚ E9 ✉ 150 N. Dearborn Street ☎ 312/422-0150
ⓜ Brown, Orange Lines: Clark/Lake 🚌 156

POTBELLY SANDWICH WORKS ($)

www.potbelly.com
There are many branches of this soup, salads and sandwiches chain downtown, and it's rightly praised for its freshly-prepared top-value dishes.
✚ E10 ✉ 209 S. La Salle Street ☎ 312/269-1684
ⓜ Brown, Orange Lines: Quincy 🚌 1, 22, 60, 151

RHAPSODY ($$$)

www.rhapsodychicago.com
Adjoining Symphony Center, the elegant Rhapsody feeds music fans modern seafood, pastas and steaks.
✚ F10 ✉ 65 E. Adams Street ☎ 312/786-9911 ⏰ No lunch Sat–Sun ⓜ Brown, Orange Lines: Adams 🚌 144, 146

RUSSIAN TEA TIME ($$)

www.russianteatime.com
Caviar, roast pheasant, iced vodka and other Russian specialties.
✚ F10 ✉ 77 E. Adams Street ☎ 312/360-0000
ⓜ Brown, Orange Lines: Adams 🚌 1, 7, 60, 126, 151

RUTH'S CHRIS STEAKHOUSE ($$–$$$)

www.ruthschris.com
The Chicago branch of the big US steak house chain

FOR VEGETARIANS

Most Chinese, Thai and Vietnamese restaurants offer meat-free versions of their staples, as do Indian eateries; Italian restaurants are another likely possibility. Even amid the chop houses and barbecued rib joints, there's usually some selection. Among the almost exclusively vegetarian restaurants try Chicago Diner (✉ 3411 N. Halsted Street ☎ 773/935-6696) and Dharma Garden Thai (✉ 3109 W. Irving Park Road ☎ 773/588-9140).

opened in 1992 and quickly made its mark. It serves substantial steaks, lamb, veal and pork, all topped with sizzling butter.
✚ E9 ✉ 431 N. Dearborn Street ☎ 312/321-2725
⏰ Dinner only Sat–Sun ⓜ Red Line: Washington 🚌 22, 36

SEVEN ON STATE ($)

On the seventh floor of Macy's, this upscale food court includes Mexican and Asian kiosks, as well as soups, salads and sandwiches. A more modest version is in the lower level food court.
✚ F9 ✉ 111 N. State Street ☎ 312/781-3693 ⓜ Red Line: Washington 🚌 29

SOUTH WATER KITCHEN ($$$)

www.southwaterkitchen.com
Inside the Hotel Monaco, South Water Kitchen is all about classic American fare such as macaroni and cheese and, on Friday, fried fish.
✚ F9 ✉ 225 N. Wabash Avenue ☎ 312/236-9300
ⓜ Red Line: Lake; Brown, Green, Orange Lines: State 🚌 29

TRATTORIA NO. 10 ($$$)

www.trattoriaten.com
This subterranean pasta specialist regularly draws sell-out crowds.
✚ E9 ✉ 10 N. Dearborn Street ☎ 312/984-1718
⏰ No lunch Sat; closed Sun ⓜ Blue Line: Washington 🚌 29

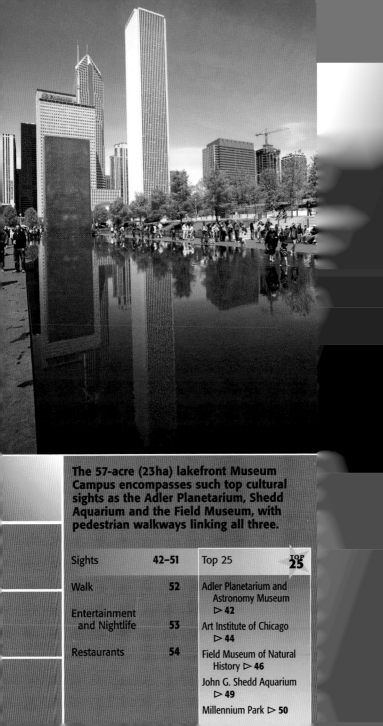

The 57-acre (23ha) lakefront Museum Campus encompasses such top cultural sights as the Adler Planetarium, Shedd Aquarium and the Field Museum, with pedestrian walkways linking all three.

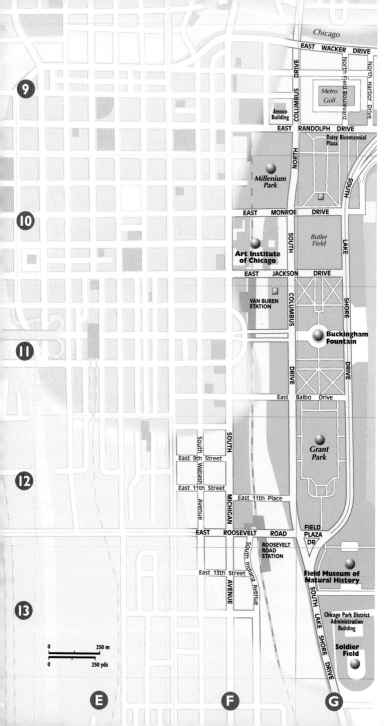

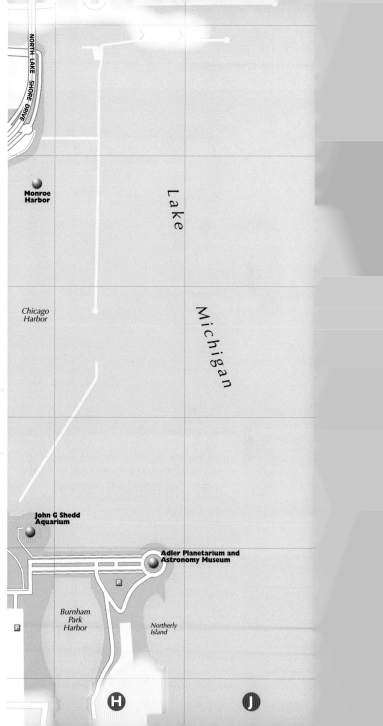

NORTH LAKE SHORE DRIVE

Monroe
Harbor

Lake

Chicago
Harbor

Michigan

John G Shedd
Aquarium

Adler Planetarium and
Astronomy Museum

P

Burnham
Park
Harbor

Northerly
Island

P

H

J

HIGHLIGHTS

- Sky Theater
- Definiti Space Theater
- Gateway to the Universe
- Martian rocks
- Looping 3-D film on galaxy creation

TIPS

- Be prepared to pay the two-show entry fee to experience the Adler in full.
- Visitors are drawn to the razzle dazzle of the Definiti Space Theater, but the Sky Theater's re-creation of the sky is more educational.

Projecting the night sky on an overhead dome (68ft/21m), Sky Theater has helped the Adler Planetarium and Astronomy Museum to win local hearts since it opened in 1930.

Skywatching Max Adler, a Sears Roebuck executive, realized his ambition to put the wonders of the cosmos within the reach of ordinary people when he provided the money to have the western hemisphere's first modern planetarium built in Chicago. The planetarium holds one of the world's major astronomical collections. This landmark building is a dodecahedron in rainbow granite, decorated with signs of the zodiac and topped by a lead-covered copper dome. The fascinating Sky Theater examines constellations and planets as they appear in the current night sky, projected

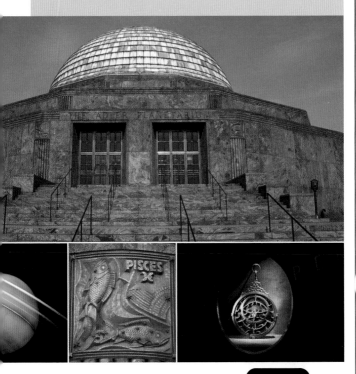

Clockwise from left: Detail of an exhibit; the exterior of the landmark Adler Planetarium building; details of exhibits and a relief

onto an overhead dome. The Definiti Space Theater uses digital technology and three-dimensional graphics to journey into space. Adler After Dark is an adult-only evening event, every third Thursday, with telescope viewing and more.

Finding space Among the permanent exhibits, Universe In Your Hands documents the early earth-centered view of the universe, bolstered by a selection of medieval telescopes. The new Planet Xplorers is a space exploration experience for kids. Other areas are devoted to how changing perceptions of the universe affected human culture, and the practicalities of exploring space, with items from manned exploration and samples of moon and Martian rock. "Shoot For The Moon" includes "A Journey with Jim Lovell," which features the fully restored Gemini 12 spacecraft.

THE BASICS

www.adlerplanetarium.org

✚ H13

✉ 1300 S. Lake Shore Drive

☎ 312/322-7827

🕐 Mon–Fri 10–4, Sat–Sun 10–4.30 (3rd Thu of month 6pm–10pm, over 21s only). Closed Thanksgiving, Dec 25

🍴 Cafeteria

🚇 Orange Line: Roosevelt

🚉 Roosevelt Road

🚌 146

♿ Good

💰 Moderate–Expensive

Housed in a classically inspired building erected for the World's Columbian Exposition in 1893, the Art Institute has an acclaimed collection of Impressionist paintings. But its galleries showcase a lot more, from arms and armor to the original trading room of the Stock Exchange.

Masterworks The celebrated *American Gothic* by Grant Wood and Edward Hopper's moody *Nighthawks* are among the highlights of the American collections. The Impressionist galleries and European art are on level 2. No work receives greater notice and admiration than Georges Seurat's expansive *A Sunday on La Grande Jatte*, a pointillist masterpiece. Seminal works in adjacent galleries include haystacks by Claude Monet,

dancers by Edgar Degas, a self-portrait on cardboard by Vincent Van Gogh and the vibrant *Paris Street; Rainy Day* by Gustave Caillebotte. The stunning new Modern Wing houses 20th- and 21st-century modern and contemporary art.

Curiosities Everything from Chinese ceramics to Guatemalan textiles has a niche on the first floor. There is a huge collection of paperweights, and decorative art. Leave time for the stunning 1898 Trading Room of the Chicago Stock Exchange, designed by Louis Sullivan and reconstructed here. The lower level photography gallery exhibits select works from its comprehensive collection and the Thorne Miniature Rooms re-create 68 historic settings in 1-inch-to-1-foot (2.5cm-to-30cm) scale. There are also regular changing exhibitions from all over the world, and a first-rate museum shop.

THE BASICS

www.artic.edu

🕂 F10

✉ 111 S. Michigan Avenue

☎ 312/443-3600

🕐 Mon–Wed, Fri 10.30–5, Thu 10.30–8, Sat–Sun 10–5

🍽 Café

Ⓜ Brown and Orange Lines: Adams

🚌 3, 4, 60, 145, 147, 151

♿ Good

💵 Expensive; free Thu 5–8

❓ Free tours daily

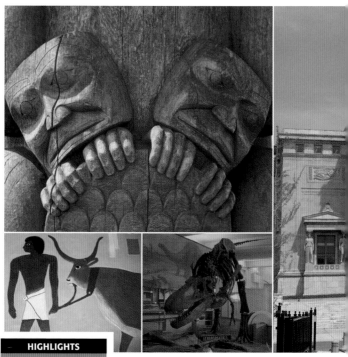

HIGHLIGHTS

● Sue
● "Traveling the Pacific"
● Dinosaur Hall
● Crown Family PlayLab
● Pawnee earth lodge
● The Ancient Americas
● World of Mammals

TIPS

● This vast museum requires a game plan on entry, and the menu of options often includes blockbuster touring exhibitions.
● In fair weather take a breather on the front or back steps with other picnickers.

One of the world's great natural history museums, the Field displays superb exhibits drawn from all corners of the globe. After a strenuous round of viewing, ponder the fact that only around one percent of the museum's 20 million artifacts is on display.

The building The museum was completed in 1920, its cavernous galleries providing a home for a collection originally assembled for Chicago's 1893 World's Columbian Exposition. With its porticoes, columns and beaux-arts decoration, the imposing design sits rather uneasily with the needs of a modern museum, and sometimes the many rooms of exhibits from myriad eras and cultures can make for jumbled viewing. But the building's many sequestered galleries make an adventure of

Clockwise from left: Detail of a totem pole; exterior of the museum; an Albertosaurus on display; detail of ancient Egyptian art

exploring the dinosaur galleries, the taxidermy-mad World of Mammals, the life of an underground bug and corners of quirky investigation.

Great exhibits The outstanding sections include the dinosaur exhibits in which Sue, the most complete Tyrannosaurus rex ever found, takes pride of place in the entrance hall; major ancient Egyptian artifacts, spanning 5000BC to AD300, arranged in and around the dimly lit and labyrinthine innards of a life-size, re-created tomb of a 5th-dynasty pharaoh; and "Traveling the Pacific," a powerful examination of cultural and spiritual life in Pacific cultures and the threats posed by the Western world's encroachment. Also noteworthy are the Native American displays and the gem collection, which includes pieces purchased in the 1890s from the famous Tiffany & Co jewelers.

THE BASICS

www.fieldmuseum.org

➕ G13

✉ E. Roosevelt Road at S. Lake Shore Drive

☎ 312/922-9410

🕐 Daily 9–5

🍴 Corner Bakery

🚇 Orange Line: Roosevelt

🚉 Roosevelt Road

🚌 146

♿ Good

💲 Expensive; free 2nd Mon of month

Entrance (opposite top);
dolphins (opposite below),
a Geentoo penguin (left);
a turtle (right)

TOP
25

John G. Shedd Aquarium

Chicago's "Ocean-by-the-Lake" is the world's largest indoor aquarium, enhanced by a state-of-the-art ocean-arium where dolphins and whales show off typical behaviors and a Philippine reef exhibit showcasing sharks.

Aquarium A re-created Caribbean coral reef at the core of this imposing Greek-style building is home to barracuda, moray eels, nurse sharks and other creatures, who are fed several times daily by a team of microphone-equipped divers who describe the creatures, their habits and their habitat. Around the reef, denizens of the deep waters of the world occupy geographically arranged tanks. Watch out for the false-eye flashlight fish, born with the piscine equivalent of a flashlight.

Oceanarium Dolphins and beluga whales are the star attractions here. Several times daily, the dolphins display natural skills such as "spy-hopping," when a dolphin raises itself onto its tail, in a schmaltzy amphitheater show called "Fantasea." Winding nature trails lead to the lower-level windows that provide an underwater view of the dolphins and whales. You also see a colony of penguins, sea otters and hands-on exhibits. Descend by elevator to the Wild Reef to see fascinating tropical creatures such as sea dragons, whiptail rays and lionfish. Only a 0.25-inch (0.6cm) thick window separates visitors from 30 sharks swimming in a massive floor-to-ceiling tank, which re-creates a reef in the Philippines.

THE BASICS

www.sheddaquarium.org
⊞ G12
✉ 1200 S. Lake Shore Drive
☎ 312/939-2438
🕐 Daily 9–5 (weekends till 6), Memorial Day–Labor Day 9–6; Jun–Aug Thu till 10pm
🍴 Soundings Restaurant; snacks from stands at Bubble Net Food Court
🚇 Orange Line: Roosevelt
🚆 Roosevelt Road
🚌 146
🍴 Excellent
💰 Expensive; free on Community Discount Days (see website); other exhibits at reduced fee

HIGHLIGHTS

- Pacific white-sided dolphins
- Beluga whales
- Sea otters
- Sea anemones
- Penguins
- Turtles
- Sharks

MUSEUM CAMPUS

TOP 25

Millennium Park

Jay Pritzker Pavilion (left) and Cloud Gate by Anish Kapoor (right)

THE BASICS

www.millenniumpark.org
- F10
- 201 E. Randolph Drive
- 312/742-1168
- Park Grill, snack shop
- Brown, Green, Orange Lines: Randolph
- 127, 144, 146, 151
- Good
- Free

HIGHLIGHTS

- Jay Pritzker Pavilion
- *Cloud Gate*, Anish Kapoor
- The Crown Fountain
- BP Bridge
- Ice-skating rink
- Chase Promenade
- Boeing Galleries sculptures

This once-neglected plot (24 acres/9.7ha) of Grant Park was converted into the art-and-architecture-filled Millennium Park in 2004 to celebrate the new century, albeit four years behind schedule.

Cutting-edge culture City planner Daniel Burnham put his stamp on Grant Park in the early 1900s, giving the city an apron of green at its front door. Millennium Park updates the civic respite concept with new landmarks by design-world greats including architect Frank Gehry, who brought his signature swooping-titanium style to the erection of the park's central theater, the Jay Pritzker Pavilion. Gehry also designed the winding bridge (308yd/281m) that leads parkgoers lake-ward. The Crown Fountain's twin glass towers (50ft/15m) project video images of a cross section of Chicagoans in portrait, while in summer children run beneath the water jets. Plazas, promenades, gardens and a restaurant with a large outdoor café in summer provide more diversion.

The Bean Briton Anish Kapoor created the 110-ton elliptical sculpture *Cloud Gate*, known locally as "the Bean." Its highly polished surface bends and warps the surrounding skyline in reflection, a sight that commonly attracts photographers. Briefly, the city tried to block shutterbugs from capturing its image, claiming copyright infringement. Public uproar duly followed and officials relented, though the city maintains that anyone seeking to publish images of the Bean needs the permission of the artist.

More to See

BUCKINGHAM FOUNTAIN
Among the features of Grant Park is the 1926 Buckingham Fountain, notable for its computer-choreographed display of colorful lights dancing on the 1.5 million gallons (6.8 million liters) of water that are pumped daily.
🚇 G11 ✉ Grant Park

GRANT PARK
Planned by Daniel Burnham in 1909 as the centerpiece of a series of lakefront parks, Grant Park is a major festival venue that has seen everything from an infamous violence-marred 1968 anti-Vietnam War demonstration to a papal Mass in 1979. Far from being a bucolic extravaganza, Grant Park is essentially a succession of lawns crisscrossed by walkways and split in two by busy Lake Shore Drive. Bordered by the high-rises of the Loop and the expanses of Lake Michigan, Grant Park never lets you forget that you are in Chicago. Its Petrillo Music Shell provides a setting for summer concerts.
🚇 G12 ✉ Bordered by S. Michigan

Avenue, E. Randolph Drive, E. Roosevelt Road and Lake Michigan 🎵 Petrillo Music Shell concert information: 312/742-4763 ☀ Visit during daylight hours only, except for special evening events 🚇 Brown, Orange Lines: Randolph, Madison or Adams 🚌 3, 4, 6, 38, 60, 145, 146, 147, 151, 157

MONROE HARBOR
Some 1,000 boats moor at Monroe Harbor, just across Lake Shore Drive from Grant Park. The masts and sails provide a picturesque foreground to a lakefront stroll.
🚇 G10 ✉ Grant Park

SOLDIER FIELD
www.soldierfield.net
The original 1924 colonnaded Greek Revival stadium is home to football's Chicago Bears. A controversial 2003 addition resembling a glass-and-steel spaceship set down within the classic arcade wall updated the services of the stadium and added luxury boxes.
🚇 G13 ✉ 1410 S. Museum Drive
☎ 312/235-7000 🚇 Red Line: Roosevelt
🚌 12, 127

MUSEUM CAMPUS

★

MORE TO SEE

Skyscrapers seen above lawns crossed by walkways at Grant Park

Buckingham Fountain

A Walk in the Park

A stroll through Chicago's front yard takes you to and past some of the city's best cultural attractions and mostly away from car traffic.

DISTANCE: Around 2 miles (3km) **ALLOW:** 90 minutes without museum stops

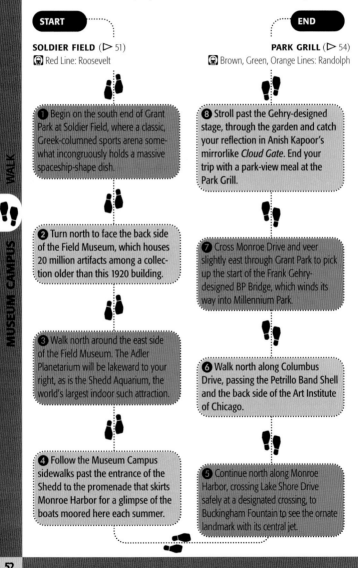

START

SOLDIER FIELD (▷ 51)
Ⓜ Red Line: Roosevelt

END

PARK GRILL (▷ 54)
Ⓜ Brown, Green, Orange Lines: Randolph

1 Begin on the south end of Grant Park at Soldier Field, where a classic, Greek-columned sports arena somewhat incongruously holds a massive spaceship-shape dish.

2 Turn north to face the back side of the Field Museum, which houses 20 million artifacts among a collection older than this 1920 building.

3 Walk north around the east side of the Field Museum. The Adler Planetarium will be lakeward to your right, as is the Shedd Aquarium, the world's largest indoor such attraction.

4 Follow the Museum Campus sidewalks past the entrance of the Shedd to the promenade that skirts Monroe Harbor for a glimpse of the boats moored here each summer.

8 Stroll past the Gehry-designed stage, through the garden and catch your reflection in Anish Kapoor's mirrorlike *Cloud Gate*. End your trip with a park-view meal at the Park Grill.

7 Cross Monroe Drive and veer slightly east through Grant Park to pick up the start of the Frank Gehry-designed BP Bridge, which winds its way into Millennium Park.

6 Walk north along Columbus Drive, passing the Petrillo Band Shell and the back side of the Art Institute of Chicago.

5 Continue north along Monroe Harbor, crossing Lake Shore Drive safely at a designated crossing, to Buckingham Fountain to see the ornate landmark with its central jet.

WALK

MUSEUM CAMPUS

Entertainment and Nightlife

JAY PRITZKER PAVILION

www.grantparkmusicfestival.com

From June to August the Grant Park Music Festival holds free classical, jazz and pop concerts on Wednesday, Friday and Saturday evenings. The Grant Park Orchestra and visiting guests play to 7,000 on the lawn and another 4,000 seated.

✚ G9 ✉ 205 E. Randolph Drive ☎ 312/742-7638 🚇 Brown, Green, Orange Lines: Randolph 🚌 127, 144, 146, 151

JOAN W. AND IRVING B. HARRIS THEATER FOR MUSIC AND DANCE

www.harristheaterchicago.org

GRANT PARK'S BLUES AND JAZZ

Each June and September the Petrillo Music Shell in Grant Park (▷ 51) is the stage for blues and jazz festivals respectively, which draw top international names as well as the city's greats in both fields. The performers are greeted by tens of thousands of fans, who arrive with blankets and picnic supplies to enjoy the free music.

The smaller of Millennium Park's entertainment venues, Harris hosts a 1,500-seat theater devoted primarily to performances of both local and visiting dance troupes.

✚ G9 ✉ 205 E. Randolph Drive ☎ 312/334-7777 🚇 Brown, Green, Orange Lines: Randolph 🚌 127, 144, 146, 151

LOLLAPALOOZA

www.lollapalooza.com

This popular three-day music festival in summer draws people from around the world to sample music from rock, alternative, hip-hop and punk music. Dance, comedy and crafts are also part of the festival, as is Kidzapolooza, an area with kids' rock concerts and music activities.

✚ G12 ✉ Grant Park 🚇 Brown, Orange Lines: Randolph, Madison or Adams ☎ 888/512-7469 (tickets) 🚌 3, 4, 6, 38, 60, 145, 146, 147, 151, 157

MUSEUM CAMPUS

ENTERTAINMENT AND NIGHTLIFE

Restaurants

PRICES

Prices are approximate, based on a 3-course meal for one person.
$$$$ over $50
$$$ $31–$50
$$ $16–$30
$ up to $15

ARIA ($$$)

www.ariachicago.com
The menu at this trendy, precurtain spot globetrots, offering Chicago steaks, Moroccan tagines, Asian noodle dishes and Indian naan bread.

🚩 G9 ✉ 200 N. Columbus Drive ☎ 312/444-9494 Ⓡ Brown, Green, Orange, Lines: Randolph 🚌 143, 144, 145, 146, 151

CORNER BAKERY CAFÉ ($)

Tucked just off the entry exhibit hall at the Field Museum, this cafeteria-style bakery serves pre-packaged cold and made-to-order hot sandwiches, as well as pizza slices and salads. Most dishes feature the baker's signature artisan bread.

🚩 G13 ✉ 1400 S. Lake Shore Drive ☎ 312/588-1040 Ⓡ Green, Orange, Red Lines: Roosevelt 🚌 12, 127

GARDEN RESTAURANT ($$)

www.artic.edu
Elegant, white-tablecloth restaurant in the heart of the Art Institute of Chicago, overlooking the tree-filled courtyard where tables are set in fair weather. Fancy fare includes duck confit salad and creamy risotto with mascarpone cheese.

🚩 F10 ✉ 111 S. Michigan Avenue ☎ 312/553-9675 Ⓡ Brown, Green, Orange, Lines: Adams 🚌 127, 144, 146, 151

THE PALM ($$$$)

www.thepalm.com
One of the upscale Palm steak house chain serving massive steaks and chops, catering to the who's who enshrined in caricatures on the restaurant walls.

🚩 G9 ✉ 323 E. Wacker Drive ☎ 312/616-1000 Ⓡ Brown, Green, Orange Lines: Randolph 🚌 143, 144, 145, 146, 151

PARK GRILL ($$$)

www.parkgrillchicago.com
Millennium Park's signature restaurant overlooks the skating rink in winter and uses the pavilion for outdoor dining in

THE TASTE OF CHICAGO

Chicagoans love to eat and do so with gusto by the thousand at the Taste of Chicago festival, one of the city's most eagerly awaited events, which is held annually in Grant Park. For the 11 days before July 4 around 100 local restaurants dispense their creations at affordable prices from open-front stalls. Free musical entertainment keeps toes tapping.

summer. Lunch options focus on hamburgers, pastas and salads. Dinner features American classics.

🚩 F10 ✉ 11 N. Michigan Avenue ☎ 312/521-7275 Ⓡ Brown, Green, Orange, Lines: Randolph 🚌 127, 144, 146, 151

SOUNDINGS CAFÉ ($$)

www.sheddaquarium.org
Panoramic lake views wrap the family-friendly casual café at the Shedd Aquarium. Fish harvested via sustainable methods is the focus of the menu, which also uses organic, locally grown produce for simpler dishes like salads, wraps and sandwiches.

🚩 G12 ✉ 1200 S. Lake Shore Drive ☎ 312/692-3277 Ⓡ Green, Orange, Red Lines: Roosevelt 🚌 12, 127

TAVERN AT THE PARK ($$$)

www.tavernatthepark.com
Across the street from Millennium Park, the Tavern is a sophisticated place offering traditional American food with a contemporary twist, and it often features in lists of top Chicago restaurants. Try their signature Cloud Gate Martini, and one of the meat dishes for which they're renowned, like the Aged New York Strip.

🚩 F9 ✉ 30 E. Randolph Street ☎ 312/552-0070 Ⓡ Brown, Orange Lines: Madison 🚌 3, 4, 60, 145, 147, 151

Chicago's most chic shopping district, the Magnificent Mile, and priciest residential districts, including the Gold Coast, abut one another north of the Chicago River. Parks buffer the lakeshore.

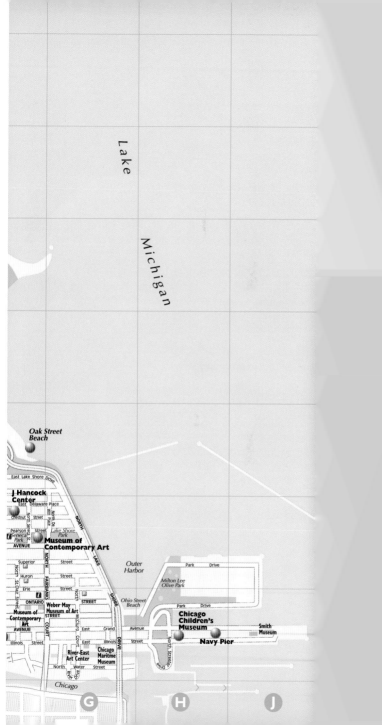

Lake

Michigan

Oak Street
Beach

East Lake Shore Drive

J Hancock
Center
East Delaware Place

North De
Witt Place

North Lake Shore Drive

Chestnut Street

Pearson Street
Seneca
Park
AVENUE

North St. Clair Street

Lake Shore
Park

Museum of
Contemporary Art

Superior Street

North

North Fairbanks Court

Huron Street

LAKE

North St. Clair Street

FAIRBANKS

Erie Street

ONTARIO STREET

Weber May
Museum of Art
STREET

Museum of
Contemporary
Art

AVENUE

North McClurg Court

North Columbus Drive

East Grand Avenue

SHORE

Outer
Harbor

Park Drive

Milton Lee
Olive Park

Ohio Street
Beach

Park Drive

Chicago
Children's
Museum

Smith
Museum

Navy Pier

Illinois Street

East Illinois Street

DRIVE

River-East
Art Center

Chicago
Maritime
Museum

North Water Street

North Streeter Drive

Chicago

G   H   J

Derek Lee pitching (opposite); home to the Chicago Cubs (left); fans at the game (right)

Attending a Ball Game at Wrigley Field

The days of successive World Series wins may be a distant memory, but the baseball of the Chicago Cubs and the defiantly unmodern form of their stadium are as much a part of Chicago as the Water Tower and the El.

Landmark With its ivy-covered brick outfield wall, Wrigley Field provides the perfect setting for America's traditional pastime. Built in 1914, the stadium has steadily resisted Astroturf, and the game takes place on grass within an otherwise ordinary city neighborhood, now known as Wrigleyville. With insufficient car-parking space, most spectators have to endure densely packed El trains to reach the ballpark. General admission bleacher seating overlooking the outfield is popular at Wrigley. Dedicated Cubs fans withstand the vagaries of Chicago weather, which during the April to October season can encompass anything from snow to sunshine and 100°F (38°C) temperatures.

Tradition Nearby residents watch the game from their windows, and some convert their roof space to boxlike seating and charge admission. Others rent out their driveways for parking. Above the seats is the much-loved 1937 scoreboard on which the numbers are moved not by computer chips but by human hands. The floodlights did not appear until 1988, and then only after a fierce campaign of resistance. Someone in a high place may have objected: The first night game was abandoned because of rain.

THE BASICS

www.chicago.cubs.mlb.com

🔲 Off map at C1

✉ 1060 W. Addison Street

☎ 773/404-2827

🎟 Games: Apr–early Oct

🍴 Fast-food stands; three restaurants

🚇 Red Line: Addison

🚌 22, 152

♿ Good

🎫 Tickets moderate to expensive

HIGHLIGHTS

● Outfield wall ivy
● Bleacher seats
● Glimpsing the game from the Addison El stop
● Hand-operated scoreboard
● Seventh inning stretch

TIP

● After the first half of the seventh inning, fans are invited to stand up and sing "Take Me Out to The Ballgame." The song is led by a celebrity, politician or sports star.

High Life at the Hancock

The Signature Room (left and right)

THE BASICS

www.signatureroom.com

➕ F7

✉ The Signature Lounge, John Hancock Center, 875 N. Michigan Avenue

☎ 312/787-9596; Observatory: 888/875-8439

🕐 Sun–Thu 11am–12.30am, Fri–Sat 11am–1.30am; Observatory: daily 9am–11pm

🍴 Appetizers and sandwiches

Ⓡ Red Line: Chicago

🚌 143, 144, 145, 146, 151

♿ Good

💲 Free; Observatory: moderate

HIGHLIGHTS

● 80-mile (129km) visibility
● Views of the skyline at night
● Martini menu
● South views from the women's bathroom
● Sunset

The perfect place to toast the city skyline is from the 96th-floor cocktail lounge in one of the skyline's stars, the 1970 John Hancock Center.

The views Solid at its base and tapering as it goes skyward, the John Hancock Center, designed by the renowned firm Skidmore, Owings and Merrill and divided nearly equally between residential and commercial use, runs a paid-admission observatory on the 94th floor (www.hancock-observatory.com). But tipplers can go higher to the Signature Lounge on the 96th floor, reached via a separate elevator with no admission charge. On a clear day visitors can see 80 miles (129km) and four surrounding states from the perch over Oak Street Beach. With unreserved seating, patrons have to dash for the best windowside seats when they become available, though all the tables have good sightlines. Sunsets draw a crowd, but it's really after sundown when the lights come up in spires all around you that the lounge is at its most romantic.

The observatory If you've children in tow, or don't want to pay the premium prices for drinks, visit the Observatory. There are fantastic views in every direction, and an open-air SkyWalk where you can feel the full blast of the Windy City. An entertaining multimedia tour, included in the admission price, highlights the skyscrapers and Chicago history. A small extra charge gets you a second admission after dark to admire the twinkling skyline.

Dozens of art dealers occupy the former warehouses in River North's most handsome district for one-stop art shopping. Tours of galleries happen on Saturday.

From industry to art Chicago's gallery district claims roughly 70 art sellers in the heart of River North bounded by Chicago Avenue on the north, the Chicago River on the south, La Salle to the east and Orleans to the west. The area boomed with industry beginning in the 1890s when railroad tracks lined the north bank of the Chicago River, earning it the nickname "Smokey Hollow." River North slid slowly into decay as factories gradually closed in the 1950s and '60s. In the 1970s, attracted by low rents and large spaces, artists began to move in. Later, galleries followed, cementing the art scene in the district of redbrick warehouse buildings. Chain restaurants and residential condos have more recently driven up rents in the area, but the galleries clustered on Huron and Superior streets in particular have managed to survive the real-estate rush.

Art scene The most established artists showing in Chicago exhibit here alongside national and international names. Maya Polsky Gallery shows works by the late Ed Paschke, Roy Boyd Gallery exhibits the abstract oils of Dan Devening and Carl Hammer Gallery displays Mr. Imagination, whose medium is bottle caps. All are open to the public but to visit with a guide, show up at Starbuck's at 750 N. Franklin Street at 11am any Saturday, where the free tours kick off.

THE BASICS

- D7
- Between the Chicago River and Chicago Avenue, La Salle and Orleans streets
- Gallery hours vary; most open Tue–Sat 10–6
- Restaurants, cafés and coffee shops nearby
- Brown Line: Chicago
- 66
- Good
- Free

HIGHLIGHTS

- Roy Boyd Gallery
- Carl Hammer Gallery
- David Weinberg Gallery
- Byron Roche Gallery
- Zolla/Lieberman Gallery
- Maya Polsky Gallery

NORTH SIDE

TOP 25

Lincoln Park Zoo

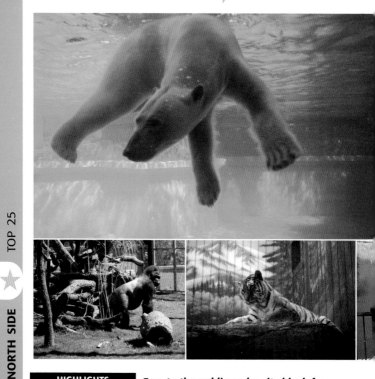

TIP

● For one of the more entertaining events at the zoo, arrive at the sea lion pool for the 2pm feeding.

Free to the public and a city block from a popular residential district, the zoo is a local favorite showcasing wild animals as well as a dairy farm, itself an endangered species in the Midwest.

Small beginnings Created out of sand dunes, swamp and the former city cemetery, Lincoln Park was established by the 1870s after its zoo had been started with the gift of two swans from New York's Central Park. Evolving over several years through the contributions of various designers, it is one of the oldest zoos in the country.

Wild kingdom The zoo, a block east of a smart residential district, is very much a part of city life where passersby can drop in on the lion pride or the swimming polar bears. Early-20th-century brick

Clockwise from left: A polar bear cooling off; the chimpanzee enclosure; giraffe; observing the seals; a tiger and a gorilla

buildings house the big cats, small mammals and some monkeys, but a spate of new building has brought more immersive exhibits to the zoo. The Regenstein African Journey creates an atmospheric passage through habitats for pygmy hippos, deer-like klipspringers, wild dogs, towering giraffes and even cockroaches. The Regenstein Center for African Apes lets the light shine into vine-covered and bamboo-planted indoor living areas, supplemented by outdoor grounds. The Children's Zoo combines play in a climbing area and education with interactive exhibits.

Down on the farm Farm-in-the-Zoo's white-trimmed red barn is one of Chicago's more unusual buildings. The farmyard attempts to teach kids where food comes from with daily presentations on milking, butter-churning and egg hatching.

THE BASICS

www.lpzoo.org

E2

2001 N. Clark Street

312/742-2000

Apr–Oct daily 10–5; Nov–Mar 10–4.30; summer weekends till 6.30

Brown Line: Fullerton

151, 156

Good

Free

Navy Pier

HIGHLIGHTS

- Ferris wheel
- Chicago Children's Museum
- Chicago Shakespeare Theater
- Boat rides
- Stained-glass window exhibit
- Views of city from the pier
- Family Pavilion Stage

TIP

- The popular beer garden at the end of the pier serves draft beer, snacks and a line-up of local bands in summer, with great skyline views.

Few visitor attractions anywhere in the world have a collection of stained-glass windows vying for attention with a 15-story Ferris wheel, but at Navy Pier they do just that, part of an expanding venue that mixes culture, cuisine, entertainment and retail.

History and cruises Opened in 1916, Navy Pier was part of architect Daniel Burnham's vision for a new Chicago and was intended to combine shipping with dining and entertainment. The former steadily disappeared and the pier declined until a 1990s makeover saw it re-emerge as a stylish family-aimed entertainment venue in the heart of the city. The pier has encouraged a revival of water activity with a plethora of pleasure cruises departing from its edge along Dock Street.

Clockwise from left: Walking along Navy Pier; looking toward Navy Pier with its Ferris wheel; Smith Museum of Stained Glass on Navy Pier; fountain outside the Children's Museum

Entertainment For thrills try the Transporter FX, a high-speed ride to the thrill of your choice, be it Antarctica, the Moon, the African wilds or the Grand Prix. The daring can ride the Wave Swinger's motorized swings spinning 14ft (4m) off the floor, while the placid can enjoy the carousel or miniature golf course.

Culture For intellectual balance, get tickets to the acclaimed Chicago Shakespeare Theater, modeled on the venues of the Bard's own day with seating surrounding the stage on three levels. Exactly 150 stained-glass windows line the pier hallways, comprising the Smith Museum of Stained Glass Windows, with superior selections by Louis Comfort Tiffany as well as Prairie School-era works. The Chicago Children's Museum educates as it entertains (▷ 69).

THE BASICS

www.navypier.com

✚ H8

✉ 600 E. Grand Avenue

☎ 312/595-5282

🕐 Summer: Fri–Sat 10am–midnight, Sun–Thu 10–10; shorter hours in winter

🍴 Various restaurants and cafés

🚊 Red Line: Grand

🚌 29, 56, 65, 66

♿ Good

🎟 Free; fee for individual attractions

North Avenue Beach

Outdoor activities at North Avenue Beach

THE BASICS

www.chicagoparkdistrict.com

➕ F4

✉ 1603 N. Lake Shore Drive

☎ 312/742-7529

🚇 Red Line: Clark Street

🚌 72

♿ Fair

🆓 Free

HIGHLIGHTS

● Beach volleyball
● Chess Pavilion
● Ocean-liner bathhouse
● Upper-deck Castaways Bar & Grill
● Seasonal outdoor gym
● Swimming

Daily in summer, and especially on weekends and holidays, Chicagoans storm this beach, one of the liveliest and best equipped of the city's 33 strands on the 31-mile (50km) Lake Michigan shore.

Games for all For a look at Chicagoans of every stripe and how they relax, head to North Avenue Beach, a community playground for families, young singles, exercise fanatics and sybarites. The park is known as a volleyballer's delight, lined with net uprights (players provide the nets and balls) used by teams as well as casual pick-up players. A temporary stadium showcases professional players when they come to town in July. Brainy sorts head to the Chess Pavilion on the concrete biking and walking path south of the beach. Each summer a seasonal outdoor gym provides weights and exercise equipment for the body proud. While you can watch Chicago's annual August Air and Water Show from a number of beaches up and down the shore, the main action takes place at North Avenue, drawing the lion's share of the million people a day who view the boat and airplane displays.

Bathhouse The ocean-liner-looking building beached on the shore replaced the original landmark Depression-era bathhouse of the same design. The 2000 version has showers, restrooms and concession stands as well as beach chair, bike and volleyball equipment rentals. Singles go to Castaways Bar & Grill for margaritas and beer, though it serves salads and sandwiches.

Detail of the exterior (left); outside the theater (middle and right)

Second City

From the stage at Second City, Chicago performers, including some very famous cast members, popularized a form of improvised comedy now seen on television and in cities around the world.

Their laurels Chicago's signature brand of bold, broad and quick wit was nurtured and became popular at Second City. Since 1959 the Old Town comedy theater has been training actors such as *Saturday Night Live* cast members John Belushi, Bill Murray and Gilda Radner. Other alumni who have passed through the theater and on to lucrative film gigs include Dan Ackroyd, Mike Myers of *Austin Powers* fame and *40 Year-Old Virgin* actor Steve Carell. Shows bear names like "Iraqtile Dysfunction" and "Truth, Justice, or the American Way," riffing on current events, pop culture and the American political scene.

Improv comedy Improvisational comedy uses no script, relying instead on the actors to supply the dialog and the direction. They call for audience suggestions and incorporate those into the action in a form known as "spot improv," popular at Second City. Theater historians trace improv back to early Europe's Commedia del'Arte in which theater troupes traveled from town to town performing in public squares and improvising the script based on a theme. With thought to making theater more generally accessible, a group of actors founded The Compass in 1950s' Chicago, which later became Second City and went on to influence performers worldwide.

THE BASICS

www.secondcity.com
- E4
- 161 N. Wells Street
- 312/337-3992
- Tue–Thu 8, Fri–Sat 8 and 11, Sun 7
- Red Line: Clark Street
- 72, 156
- Fair
- Expensive

HIGHLIGHTS

- Improv shows
- Cabaret seating
- Two stages
- Central Old Town location near restaurants and bars

Shoppers orienting themselves and walking (left and right); Tiffany's (middle)

THE BASICS

www.themagnificentmile.com

F8

Michigan Avenue north of the Chicago River to its terminus at Oak Street

312/642-3570

Red Line: Chicago, Grand

143, 144, 145, 146, 151

Good

HIGHLIGHTS

- Water Tower and Pumping Station
- Bloomingdale's
- Nordstrom
- Saks Fifth Avenue
- Crate & Barrel
- Ralph Lauren

From the Chicago River to Oak Street Beach, that portion of Michigan Avenue known as Chicago's Magnificent Mile lines up designer boutiques and major department stores in one bustling stretch.

Shop till you drop Over 460 stores pack the mile, selling something for everyone from designer goods by Salvatore Ferragamo, precious jewelry at Cartier and the tailored suits of Brooks Brothers to off-price fashions from Swedish retailer H&M. Between high and low ends are the major American department stores, including Nordstrom, known for its quality clothes and fine shoe selection; Neiman Marcus, famed for its exclusive clientele and designer racks; and Bloomingdale's, with trendy looks for each family member. Vertical malls such as 900 North Michigan, which houses Bloomingdale's, and Water Tower Place, home to a branch of Macy's, house specialty shops such as cook's favorite Williams-Sonoma and Coach leatherware. Mothers and daughters flock to American Girl Place, a doll store with accessories.

Culture breaks Architectural icons line the street, making this a good walk even for the shop shy. The Wrigley Building and the Chicago Tribune Building face off against one another on the south end of the street. Farther north, the historic Water Tower and Pumping Station, two of the few to survive the Great Fire of 1871, symbolize the rebirth of the city on the prosperous thoroughfare. A block from Michigan Avenue, the Museum of Contemporary Art shows cutting-edge work.

More to See

BOY'S TOWN

www.northalsted.com
The pocket of Lakeview around North Halsted Street from Belmont north to Addison is the locus of the gay community in Chicago, with a lively collection of bars, shops and restaurants.

➕ Off map at C1 ✉ Halsted Street from Belmont north to Addison 🚇 Red Line: Belmont Addison; Brown Line: Belmont 🚌 8, 77 ♿ Good

CHICAGO CHILDREN'S MUSEUM

www.chicagochildrensmuseum.org
Three floors of scores of lively and entertaining things to do for those under 12. These include workshop areas such as the Inventing Lab, where children can assemble flying machines, and Artabounds, where they can create their own murals and sculptures. Programs change daily.

➕ H8 ✉ Navy Pier, 700 E. Grand Avenue ☎ 312/527-1000 🕐 Daily 10–5 (till 8 on Thu) 🚇 Red Line: Grand 🚌 29, 56, 65, 66 ♿ Good 💷 Moderate; free Thu 5–8

CHICAGO HISTORY MUSEUM

www.chicagohs.org
In a Georgian-style brick building constructed in 1932, with a modern, glass-walled extension, every major facet in Chicago's rise from swampland to metropolis is discussed and illustrated in chronologically arranged galleries. Alongside temporary shows, the American Wing houses exhibitions that explore US history via informative texts and excellent period items.

➕ E4 ✉ 1601 N. Clark Street ☎ 312/642-4600 🕐 Mon–Sat 9.30–4.30, Sun 12–5 🚇 Brown Line: Sedgwick 🚌 11, 22, 36, 72, 151, 156 ♿ Good 💷 Moderate; free Mon

FOURTH PRESBYTERIAN CHURCH

www.fourthchurch.org
This Gothic Revival church (1914) serves a congregation of Chicago's moneyed elite. Occasional but enjoyable lunchtime concerts pack the pews.

➕ F7 ✉ 126 E. Chestnut Street ☎ 312/787-4570 🚇 Red Line: Chicago 🚌 145, 146, 147, 151 ♿ Good

Chicago Children's Museum

Rail tickets displayed at Chicago History Museum

THE GOLD COAST

In the late 19th century, Chicago businessman Potter Palmer astonished his peers by erecting a mansion home on undeveloped land well north of the Loop close to Lake Michigan. As others followed, the area became known as the Gold Coast, its streets lined by the elegant homes of the well-to-do.
✚ F5

GRACELAND CEMETERY

www.gracelandcemetery.org
Graceland is Chicago's most prestigious cemetery. Alongside great Chicagoans are a host of others, famous and infamous. City architect Louis Sullivan has left a mark with his ornate 1890 tomb for the steel magnate Henry Getty and his family. Sullivan is here, as are other Chicago architects Daniel Burnham, John Root and modernist Ludwig Mies van der Rohe. The free map from the office is essential.
✚ Off map at C1 ✉ 4001 N. Clark Street
☎ 773/525-1105 🕐 Office: Mon–Sat 8.30–4.30. Gates: 8–4.30 🚇 Brown Line: Irving Park. Red Line: Sheridan 🚌 80 ♿ Good 🖐 Free

HISTORIC WATER TOWER

This pseudo-Gothic confection in yellow limestone, built in 1869 by William Boyington, is a city landmark.
✚ F7 ✉ 806 N. Michigan Avenue
☎ First-floor photography gallery: 312/742-0808 🕐 Mon–Sat 10–6.30, Sun 10–5
🚇 Red Line: Chicago 🚌 3, 66, 145, 146, 147, 151 ♿ Few 🖐 Free

HOLY NAME CATHEDRAL

www.holynamecathedral.org
This is the atmospheric seat of the Catholic Archdiocese of Chicago (1878). Bullets from the 1926 gangland murder of mobster "Hymie" Weiss chipped the building's cornerstone.
✚ F7 ✉ 735 N. State Street ☎ 312/787-8040 🚇 Red Line: Chicago 🚌 29, 36
♿ Good

INTERNATIONAL MUSEUM OF SURGICAL SCIENCES

www.imss.org
The museum's several floors, as well

The Hall of Mortals at the International Museum of Surgical Sciences

Historic Water Tower

as innovative temporary shows, cover health and medicine-related subjects. Among the oldest exhibits are drilled skulls from Peruvian temples, and surgeon's tools found in excavations at the Roman town of Pompeii. Many rooms are packed with displays of fearsome needles, hooks and other sharp metallic things.

✚ F5 ✉ 1524 N. Lake Shore Drive ☎ 312/642-6502 🕐 Tue–Sat 10–4 (also May–Sep Sun 10–4) 🚇 Brown Line: Sedgwick 🚌 151 ♿ Good 💵 Moderate; free on Tue ❓ Guided tour Sat 2pm

LINCOLN PARK CONSERVATORY

The Conservatory (1891) encompasses four separate greenhouses. Invitingly warm on cool and breezy Chicago days, the greenhouses provide balmy temperatures for dazzling tropical and subtropical blooms and seasonal displays.

✚ E2 ✉ 2391 N. Stockton Drive ☎ Conservatory: 312/742-7736 🕐 Daily 9–5 ♿ Good 🚇 Red Line: Armitage 🚌 76, 77, 145, 146, 147, 151, 156 💵 Free

MUSEUM OF CONTEMPORARY ART

www.mcachicago.org

Highlights from the permanent collection include the works of Chicago-based Ed Paschke, and Richard Long's *Chicago Mud Circle* (1996), created directly on a gallery wall. The lower levels house temporary exhibitions and provide access to the Sculpture Garden. A guide can take you on a free tour of the exhibitions and collection.

✚ F7 ✉ 220 E. Chicago Avenue ☎ 312/280-2660 🕐 Tue 10–8, Wed–Sun 10–5 🍴 Café 🚇 Red Line: Chicago 🚌 157 ♿ Good 💵 Moderate; free on Tue ❓ Guided tours daily (45 min)

OAK STREET BEACH

The closeness of the exclusive Gold Coast neighborhood helps make Oak Street Beach the gathering place for some of Chicago's richest and best-toned bodies.

✚ F6 ✉ Access from junction of N. Michigan Avenue and E. Lake Shore Drive 🚌 145, 146, 147, 151

Bust of the conductor Sir Georg Solti outside the Conservatory in Lincoln Park

OLD TOWN
www.oldtownchicago.org
Gentrified in the 1960s and '70s by
artists, Old Town combines restaurant-
lined commercial throughways and
intimate leafy residential streets. The
annual June art fair is a big draw.
✚ D5 ✉ Streets fan out from intersection
of North Avenue and Wells Street 🚇 Brown
Line: Sedgwick 🚌 11, 72, 156

THE PEGGY NOTEBAERT
NATURE MUSEUM
www.naturemuseum.org
Lively exhibits explore the natural
history of the Midwest, including a
greenhouse holding Butterfly Haven,
and the inside story on the insect
population of every household.
✚ E2 ✉ On banks of North Pond in
Lincoln Park ☎ 773/755-5100 🕐 Mon–Fri
9–4.30, Sat–Sun 10–5 🚇 Brown and Red
Lines: Fullerton 🚌 22, 36, 72, 156
♿ Good 💵 Moderate; donations

THE TRIBUNE TOWER
In the 1920s, the *Chicago Tribune*
staged a competition for the design of
its new premises. The resulting neo-
Gothic building is best admired from
the exterior, inlaid with 120 stones
from sites around the world including
Greece's Parthenon and India's Taj
Mahal. You can watch WGN, the
Tribune-owned radio station, through
the studio window.
✚ F8 ✉ 435 N. Michigan Avenue
☎ 312/222-9100 🚇 Red Line: Grand 🚌 3,
11, 29, 65, 147, 151, 157 ♿ Good

THE WRIGLEY BUILDING
The Wrigley Building was partly modeled on the Giralda Tower in Seville,
Spain, although the ornamental features echo the French Renaissance.
The North and South buildings stand
behind a continuous facade linked by
an arcaded walkway at street level and
by two enclosed aerial walkways. The
ornate glazed terra-cotta facade has
retained its original gleam; most effec-
tive when illuminated at night.
✚ F8 ✉ 400 N. Michigan Avenue
☎ 312/923-8080 🕐 Business hours
🚇 Red Line: Grand 🚌 3, 11, 29, 65, 147,
151, 157 ♿ Good 💵 Free

The Wrigley Building

*The ornate entrance to the
Tribune Tower*

One Magnificent Walk

Take in several architectural icons as well as the glitziest shopping in a mile-long walk up Michigan Avenue from the Chicago River.

DISTANCE: 1 mile (1.6 km) **ALLOW:** 2–3 hours

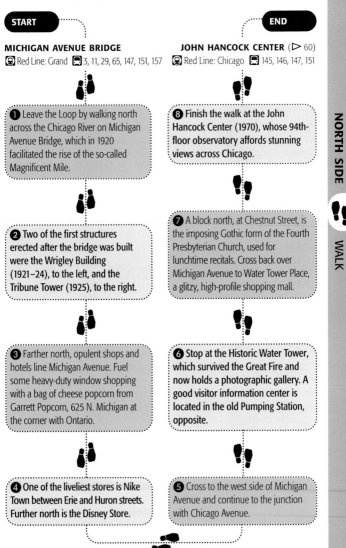

START

MICHIGAN AVENUE BRIDGE
🚇 Red Line: Grand 🚌 3, 11, 29, 65, 147, 151, 157

END

JOHN HANCOCK CENTER (▷ 60)
🚇 Red Line: Chicago 🚌 145, 146, 147, 151

❶ Leave the Loop by walking north across the Chicago River on Michigan Avenue Bridge, which in 1920 facilitated the rise of the so-called Magnificent Mile.

❽ Finish the walk at the John Hancock Center (1970), whose 94th-floor observatory affords stunning views across Chicago.

❷ Two of the first structures erected after the bridge was built were the Wrigley Building (1921–24), to the left, and the Tribune Tower (1925), to the right.

❼ A block north, at Chestnut Street, is the imposing Gothic form of the Fourth Presbyterian Church, used for lunchtime recitals. Cross back over Michigan Avenue to Water Tower Place, a glitzy, high-profile shopping mall.

❸ Farther north, opulent shops and hotels line Michigan Avenue. Fuel some heavy-duty window shopping with a bag of cheese popcorn from Garrett Popcorn, 625 N. Michigan at the corner with Ontario.

❻ Stop at the Historic Water Tower, which survived the Great Fire and now holds a photographic gallery. A good visitor information center is located in the old Pumping Station, opposite.

❹ One of the liveliest stores is Nike Town between Erie and Huron streets. Further north is the Disney Store.

❺ Cross to the west side of Michigan Avenue and continue to the junction with Chicago Avenue.

NORTH SIDE

WALK

Shopping

900 NORTH MICHIGAN
www.shop900.com
This gleaming marble high-rise consumes a city block. Restaurants, cinemas and stores are grouped around a six-floor atrium; a branch of Bloomingdale's is an anchor. There are also smaller, exclusive stores.
F7 ⊠ 900 N. Michigan Avenue ☎ 312/915-3916 Red Line: Chicago 145, 146, 147, 151

AMERICAN GIRL PLACE
www.americangirl.com
At this popular doll store in Water Tower Place, you can not only buy a doll that looks like you; also get her hair styled, take her to tea and have your photos taken for the cover of a souvenir magazine.
F7 ⊠ 835 N. Michigan Avenue ☎ 877/247-5223 Red Line: Chicago 33, 143, 144, 145, 146, 147, 148, 151, X3

BANANA REPUBLIC
www.bananarepublic.com
Popular local branch of the supplier of quality casualwear. Other stores at 835 N. Michigan and 900 N. Michigan.
F8 ⊠ 744 N. Michigan Avenue ☎ 312/642-0020 Red Line: Chicago 145, 146, 147, 151

BARNEYS NEW YORK
www.barneys.com
Branch of a Manhattan store noted for chic women's clothing and its fine menswear.
F6 ⊠ 15 E. Oak Street ☎ 312/587-1700 Red Line: Chicago 145, 146, 147, 151

BOURDAGE PEARLS
www.bourdagepearls.com
It's worth the journey to this northside jewelry gallery near Wrigley Field for its high-quality fresh-water pearls in a variety of colors. Beautiful yet affordable.
Off map C1 ⊠ 3530 N. Southport Avenue ☎ 773/244-1126 Brown Line: Southport 152

BROOKS BROTHERS
www.brooksbrothers.com
Well-made menswear, in conservative styles, plus some equally straightforward clothing for women.

KEEPING YOUR MARBLES
Anyone who thinks shopping is a mindless exercise has yet to visit Marbles: The Brain Store. It's full of fun and challenging games, books, puzzles and products that aim to sharpen your memory and critical thinking, improve your coordination and creativity, and strengthen your brain power. From magnetic Buckyballs to sophisticated brain software, there's something for everyone; try out many products in-store. There are two Chicago locations: 55 E. Grand Avenue and 4745 N. Lincoln Avenue; www. marblesthebrainstore.com.

F8 ⊠ 713 N. Michigan Avenue ☎ 312/915-0060 Red Line: Chicago 145, 146, 147, 151

CHICAGO PLACE
www.chicago-place.com
A branch of Saks Fifth Avenue department store is an anchor tenant among the classy retailers in this towering construction. Top floor food hall.
F8 ⊠ 700 N. Michigan Avenue ☎ 312/672-4811 Red Line: Chicago 145, 146, 147, 151

THE DAISY SHOP
www.daisyshop.com
Gloves, handkerchiefs and jewelry feature among the used designer accessories; also shelves of flowing chiffon dresses.
F6 ⊠ 67 E. Oak Street ☎ 312/943-8880 Red Line: Chicago 145, 146, 147, 151

ELEMENTS
www.elementschicago.com
From home decor to handbags, jewelry and fashion accessories, this treasure house of style and design features beautiful objects from around the world.
E7 ⊠ 741 N. Wells Street ☎ 877/642-6574 Brown, Purple Lines: Chicago 66, 156

HERSHEY'S CHICAGO
www.hersheys.com/discover/chicago.asp
Every imaginable size and variety of Hershey's chocolate is sold at this

fun retail store and bakery. Shop for souvenirs or play factory worker.
🔵 F7 ✉ 822 N. Michigan Avenue ☎ 312/337-7711
🔴 Red Line: Chicago 🚌 145, 146, 147, 151

J. CREW
www.jcrew.com
Classic modern clothes, shoes and accessories for young men and women at work and play.
🔵 F7 ✉ 900 N. Michigan Avenue ☎ 312/751-2739
🔴 Red Line: Chicago 🚌 145, 146, 147, 151

NAVY PIER
www.navypier.com
Around 40 shops are gathered in this complex of restaurants and entertainment venues. If you want souvenirs as gifts, this is a good place.
🔵 H8 ✉ 700 E. Grand Avenue ☎ 312/595-7437
🔴 Red Line: Grand 🚌 29, 56, 65, 66

NEIMAN-MARCUS
www.neimanmarcus.com
Exclusive, elegant clothing is the forte of this store, which also sells beauty products and fancy food stuffs. Just looking is fun.
🔵 F8 ✉ 737 N. Michigan Avenue ☎ 312/642-5900
🔴 Red Line: Chicago 🚌 145, 146, 147, 151

P.O.S.H.
www.poshchicago.com
The expression "port out/starboard home" used by aristocrats seeking the shady side of the

ship journeying between Britain and India lends its name to this antiques shop specializing in vintage tabletop items from the early 19th century.
🔵 F8 ✉ 613 N. State Street ☎ 312/280-1602 🔴 Red Line: Grand 🚌 22, 65

PRADA
www.prada.com
Three levels of designer clothing and accessories.
🔵 F6 ✉ 30 E. Oak Street ☎ 312/951-1113 🔴 Red Line: Chicago 🚌 145, 146, 147, 151

R. H. LOVE GALLERIES
www.rhlovegalleries.com
For decades Chicago's leading purveyor of fine American paintings and prints; even if the purchase of an original is beyond your means, admire the displays and frequent exhibitions.

MAGNIFICENT MILE
No Chicago shopper could be unaware that most top-class stores are gathered along the section of Michigan Avenue known as the Magnificent Mile. Many stores appeared here following the 1920s opening of the river bridge linking Michigan Avenue to the Loop, but the "Magnificent Mile" concept was a 1940s idea that eventually mutated into today's rows of marble-clad towers, mostly built during the 1970s and 1980s.

🔵 F7 ✉ 645 N. Michigan Avenue, 2nd floor
☎ 800/437-7568 🔴 Red Line: Grand 🚌 3, 11, 125, 145, 146, 147, 151

SHOPS AT THE MART
www.merchandisemart.com
Most of the vast Merchandise Mart is closed to the public, except for the first two floors, which woo shoppers with clothing stores, gift shops and food court.
🔵 E9 ✉ 350 N. Wells Street ☎ 800/677-6278 🔴 Brown, Purple Lines: Merchandise Mart 🚌 37

ULTIMO
www.ultimo.com
This chic boutique with a well-edited designer selection dresses the city's fashionistas.
🔵 F6 ✉ 116 E. Oak Street ☎ 312/787-1171 🔴 Red Line: Chicago 🚌 145, 146, 147, 151

WATER TOWER PLACE
www.shopwatertower.com
Packing seven floors are clothing stores for men, women and children that span Abercrombie & Fitch, Betsy Johnson, French Connection and Victoria's Secret. There are also jewelers, art galleries, home-furnishing emporiums, cinemas and restaurants, and specialty retailers such as Accent Chicago and the Water Tower Clock Shop.
🔵 F7 ✉ 835 N. Michigan Avenue ☎ 312/440-3165
🔴 Red Line: Chicago 🚌 145, 146, 147, 151

Entertainment and Nightlife

ANDY'S JAZZ CLUB

www.andysjazzclub.com
Popular and unpretentious jazz venue that earns its keep by staging commendable sets nightly from about 4 or 5pm until late.
🚇 F8 ✉ 11 E. Hubbard Street ☎ 312/642-6805
🚊 Red Line: Grand 🚌 29, 36

THE BATON SHOW LOUNGE

www.thebatonshowlounge.com
A rowdy, cabaretlike show where female impersonators dress like celebrities and sing. The humor is bawdy, the costumes are elaborate but the singers are talented. It's nearly impossible to tell that they're actually men. A popular spot for bachelorette parties. Booking recommended.
🚇 E8 ✉ 436 N. Clark ☎ 312/ 644-5269
🚊 Red Line: Grand 🚌 22

BILLY GOAT TAVERN

www.billygoattavern.com
This below-street-level, unpretentious watering hole is a favorite among local journalists.
🚇 F8 ✉ 430 N. Michigan Avenue ☎ 312/222-1525
🚊 Red Line: Grand 🚌 145, 146, 147, 151

BLUE CHICAGO

www.bluechicago.com
Comfortable, homey blues club, showcasing home-grown musical talent.
🚇 E7 ✉ 536 N. Clark Street and 736 N. Clark Street ☎ 312/661-0100 and 312/642-6261 🚊 Red Line: Chicago 🚌 22, 36

B.L.U.E.S.

www.chicagobluesbar.com
One of the best little blues clubs in Chicago and worth the trip out, but get there early as it's a tiny venue. On Sunday nights your admission here will also get you into Kingston Mines (▷ 77).
🚇 C1 ✉ 2519 N. Halsted Street ☎ 773/528-1012
🚊 Red, Brown Lines: Fullerton 🚌 8

CHICAGO SHAKESPEARE THEATER

www.chicagoshakes.com
A 500-seat auditorium on Navy Pier makes a splendid setting for the works of the Bard. Abridged "Short Shakespeare" and family musicals in summer.
🚇 H8 ✉ 800 E. Grand

NIGHTCLUB NEWS

The most general source is the Friday edition of the *Chicago Tribune* and its Metromix website (www.metromix.com). Inside info on the latest clubs, as well as the nightlife scene in general, can be found in the pages of the weekly *Chicago Reader* and *New City*, both free of charge, and on their websites. The weekly magazine *Time Out Chicago* is sold on local newsstands.

Avenue ☎ 312/595-5600
🚊 Red Line: Grand 🚌 29, 56, 65, 66

EXCALIBUR

www.excaliburchicago.com
This complex of billiards, pinball, video games, discos and a restaurant is incongruously set in a 19th-century pseudo-Gothic castle, a granite structure built in the 1890s for the Chicago Historical Society. Popular with twenty-somethings.
🚇 E8 ✉ 632 N. Dearborn Street ☎ 312/266-1944
🚊 Red Line: Grand 🚌 22

HOUSE OF BLUES

www.hob.com
Blues and rock from around the city, the country and the world every night. The smaller Back Porch stage has blues nightly and is open at lunch for more of the same. A gospel choir stars at Sunday brunch.
🚇 E9 ✉ 329 N. Dearborn Street ☎ 312/923-2000
🚊 Red Line: Grand 🚌 22, 36, 62

JAZZ SHOWCASE

www.jazzshowcase.com
Photos of jazz legends decorate this historic joint, and big names play here. Bring the kids to the Sunday matinee.
🚇 E8 ✉ Dearborn Station, 806 S. Plymouth Court ☎ 312/360-0234 🚊 Red Line: Grand 🚌 22, 65

JOE'S BE-BOP CAFÉ

Listen to be-bop and other jazz while tucking

BLUE CHICAGO

into jambalaya, barbe-
cued ribs and other Cajun
dishes. Popular among
music fans and tourists.
➕ H8–J8 ✉ Navy Pier, 700
E. Grand Avenue ☎ 312/595-
5299 Ⓡ Red Line: Grand
🚌 29, 55, 65, 66

KINGSTON MINES
www.kingstonmines.com
Regularly voted Chicago's
best blues club, this place
has been in business
since 1968. It's way off
the track for most city visitors, so only those in the
know head out here.
➕ C1 ✉ 2548 N. Halsted
Street ☎ 773/477-4646
Ⓡ Red, Brown Lines:
Fullerton 🚌 8

LOOKINGGLASS
THEATRE
www.lookingglasstheatre.org
Housed in the Water
Tower Pumping Station,
the Lookingglass troupe is
lauded for its experimen-
tal staging and frequent
use of circus arts.
➕ F7 ✉ 821 N. Michigan
Avenue ☎ 312/337-0665
Ⓡ Red Line: Chicago 🚌 66,
143, 144, 145, 146, 151

PARK WEST
www.parkwestchicago.com
Intimate size and strong
acoustics make this the
ideal place for non-ear-
splitting music, be it folk,
jazz, rock or something
else from the eclectic
program.
➕ D3 ✉ 322 W. Armitage
Avenue ☎ 773/929-1322
Ⓡ Brown, Red Lines:
Armitage 🚌 23, 72

LE PASSAGE
www.lepassage.tv
The well-heeled toddle
down a cobblestone alley
to reach the subterranean
Le Passage, a swanky,
renovated drinking and
dancing nightspot with a
celebrity following.
➕ F7 ✉ 937 N. Rush Street
☎ 312/255-0022 Ⓡ Red
Line: Chicago 🚌 22, 66

SECOND CITY
www.secondcity.com
Biting satire and inspired
improvisation have long
been the stock-in-trade
here, and they have been
so successful that a sec-
ond Second City stage
offers a separate cast and
show (▷ 67).
➕ E5 ✉ 1616 N. Wells Street
☎ 773/337-3992 Ⓡ Brown
Line: Sedgwick 🚌 11, 156

SPY BAR
www.spybarchicago.com
Patrons dress in swanky
club gear to edge past
the bouncers, then sip
Martinis before grooving
to house music—the Spy
Bar specialty. Sink into a
velvet couch when you
need a breather. Entrance

LIQUOR LAWS
Some bars serve liquor until
2am every night except
Saturday, when they may do
so until 3am. Others continue serving until 4am (5am
on Sunday mornings). The
drinking age is 21, and stores
may not sell liquor before
noon on Sunday.

through alleyway.
➕ E7 ✉ 646 N. Franklin
Street ☎ 312/587-8779
Ⓡ Brown Line: Chicago
🚌 37

STEPPENWOLF
THEATER
www.steppenwolf.org
Home of the enormously
successful and influential
Steppenwolf repertory
company, founded in
1976, and still a premier
venue for the best of Off-
Loop theater. The theater
has a 900-seat main hall
and a smaller space for
experimental drama.
High-profile members
include John Malkovich.
➕ C4 ✉ 1650 N. Halsted
Street ☎ 312/335-1650
Ⓡ Red Line: North/Clybourn
🚌 8, 72

STONE LOTUS
www.stonelotuslounge.com
High fashion River North
club specializing in bottle
service that comes with
food planned to match
the booze. Expect
celebrities, models and
expensive tabs.
➕ D7 ✉ 873 N. Orleans
Street ☎ 312/440-9680
Ⓡ Brown Line: Chicago
🚌 66

ZANIES
www.chicago.zanies.com
Small, enjoyable comedy
club, featuring rising local
stars as well as better-
known names.
➕ E5 ✉ 1548 N. Wells
Street ☎ 312/337-4027
Ⓡ Brown Line: Sedgwick
🚌 11, 156

Restaurants

ADOBO GRILL (\$\$)

www.adobogrill.com
Authentic Mexican dishes in a convivial atmosphere just below Second City. Don't miss the guacamole, prepared tableside. Connoisseurs choose from more than 100 tequilas on offer.
🚼 E5 ✉ 1610 N. Wells Street ☎ 312/266-7999 🚇 Red Line: Clark/Division 🚌 72, 156

ALINEA (\$\$\$\$)

www.alinea-restaurant.com
Chef Grant Achatz practices a form of alchemical cooking at Alinea that incorporates science in deconstructing dishes presented on custom serving pieces such as spindles or aromatic pillows. For bold and liberal tastes only. Reservations must be made at least six weeks in advance.
🚼 C4 ✉ 1723 N. Halstead ☎ 312/867-0110 🚇 Brown Line: Armitage 🚌 8

BEN PAO (\$\$)

www.benpao.com
Inventive and inspired take on Chinese regional dishes, served under subdued lighting. "Hot pot" tables allow diners to

cook their own noodles fondue-style.
🚼 E8 ✉ 52 W. Illinois Street ☎ 312/222-1888 🚇 Red Line: Grand 🚌 36

BIG BOWL CAFÉ (\$–\$\$)

www.bigbowl.com
Delectable Chinese noodle dishes and Thai curries served in big bowls.
🚼 F6 ✉ 6 E. Cedar Street ☎ 312/640-8888 ⏰ Dinner only Sun 🚇 Brown Line: Chicago 🚌 37, 41

BIN 36 (\$–\$\$\$)

www.bin36.com
Convivial River North loft-cum-wine-bar café pours dozens of selections by the glass and in wine "flights" or tasting portions paired to French-inflected American food and a 50-offering cheese bar. Seating ranges from café tables to stools at

the zinc-topped bar.
🚼 E9 ✉ 339 N. Dearborn Street ☎ 312/755-9463 🚇 Red Line: Grand 🚌 22

BISTRO 110 (\$\$\$–\$\$\$\$)

www.levyrestaurants.com
This long-time Chicago favorite offers classic bistro fare from a great location, just off the Magnificent Mile.
🚼 F7 ✉ 110 E. Pearson Street ☎ 312/266-3110 🚇 Red Line: Chicago Avenue 🚌 145, 146, 147 151

BRASSERIE JO (\$\$–\$\$\$)

www.brasseriejo.com
The Alsace native chef cooks up French comfort food in a classic brasserie setting with tile floors, wall mirrors and waiters in long white aprons.
🚼 E8 ✉ 59 W. Hubbard Street ☎ 312/595-0800 🚇 Red Line: Grand 🚌 22

CHARLIE TROTTER'S (\$\$\$\$)

www.charlietrotters.com
Chicago top toque Charlie Trotter prepares a unique eight-course \$165 (\$135 for vegetarians) prix-fixe menu each night, drawing the finest ingredients from around the world.
🚼 C3 ✉ 816 W. Armitage Street ☎ 312/248-6228 🚇 Brown Line: Armitage 🚌 8

ED DEBEVIC'S SHORT ORDER DELUXE (\$\$)

www.eddebevics.com
Sandwiches, great burgers and milkshakes served to

the sound of 1950s and 1960s music.

 F8 ✉ 640 N. Wells Street ☎ 312/664-1707 🍴 Breakfast only weekends 🚇 Brown Line: Chicago 🚌 37, 41

FRONTERA GRILL/ TOPOLOBAMPO ($$$–$$$$)

www.fronterakitchens.com
Chef Rick Bayless introduced the nation to regional Mexican food from his Frontera Grill hot spot in River North. Adjoining Topolobampo is the fine dining counterpart to Frontera's fiesta feel; two of the city's best restaurants.

E8 ✉ 445 N. Clark Street ☎ 312/661-1434 🍴 Closed Sun–Mon 🚇 Red Line: Grand 🚌 22

GENE & GEORGETTI ($$$$)

www.geneandgeorgetti.com
Many feel that this steak house—complete with the men's-club decor, gruff waiters and deliciously thick cuts of meat—is the best in the city. Non-carnivores beware though, there's scant choice to satisfy you.

E8 ✉ 500 N. Franklin Street ☎ 312/527-3718 🍴 Closed Sun 🚇 Brown, Purple Lines: Merchandise Mart 🚌 37

GRAND LUX CAFÉ ($$–$$$)

www.grandluxcafe.com
With a breathtakingly opulent and spacious interior, the Lux serves up a truly international menu, from Jamaican jerk chicken to veal saltimbocca. Whether you want a tasty meal or just a break from Magnificent Mile shopping with a salad or a sandwich, the Lux is hard to beat.

F8 ✉ 600 N. Michigan Avenue ☎ 312/276-2500 🚇 Red Line: Grand 🚌 143, 144, 145, 146, 151

MAGGIANO'S LITTLE ITALY ($$–$$$)

www.maggianos.com
One of the best and yet best-value Italians in town, which manages to be both smart yet informal, and always busy. Try the baked *ziti* (a type of pasta) and sausage or lobster ravioli.

E8 ✉ 516 N. Clark Street ☎ 312/644-7700 🚇 Red Line: Grand 🚌 22, 65

PIZZA!

Chicago is where the deep-dish pizza was invented, but just who invented it is open to debate. One contender as creator of this deep-crusted doubly-thick style of pizza is Gino's East (several locations including ✉ 162 E. Superior Street ☎ 312/266-3337), but Pizzeria Uno (✉ 29 E. Ohio Street ☎ 312/321-1000) also claims to have been first. Stuffed pizzas, with a crust top and bottom, are also a Chicago specialty. For this, try Giordano's (✉ 730 N. Rush Street ☎ 312/951-0747 and other locations).

MORTON'S OF CHICAGO ($$$)

www.mortons.com
Chicago takes steak seriously, and this is one of the best places to eat it. Porterhouses grilled to perfection are the stock-in-trade.

E7 ✉ 1050 N. State Street ☎ 312/266-4820 🍴 Dinner only 🚇 Red Line: Chicago 🚌 36

RIVA ($$$)

www.rivanavypier.com
Riva can claim to be Chicago's only seafood restaurant that's on the waterfront, with views of the city skyline and Lake Michigan. Though dishes like lobster, king crab, salmon and halibut are unsurprisingly popular, Riva also does good steaks in a light and bright smart-casual room.

H8 ✉ Navy Pier, 700 E. Grand Avenue ☎ 312/644-7482 🚇 Red Line: Grand 🚌 9, 56, 65, 66

ROSEBUD ON RUSH ($$$)

www.rosebudrestaurants.com
With casual dining and a bar downstairs, and a more formal restaurant upstairs, Rosebud serves up huge helpings of Italian fare like eggplant parmesan or a daily risotto dish, at this and several other city locations.

F7 ✉ 720 N. Rush Street ☎ 312/266-6444 🚇 Red Line: Chicago 🚌 66

Perhaps the city's most history-rich quarter, the South Side hosted the first mansions in Chicago and the 1983 World's Columbian Exposition, and later welcomed black immigrants from the south.

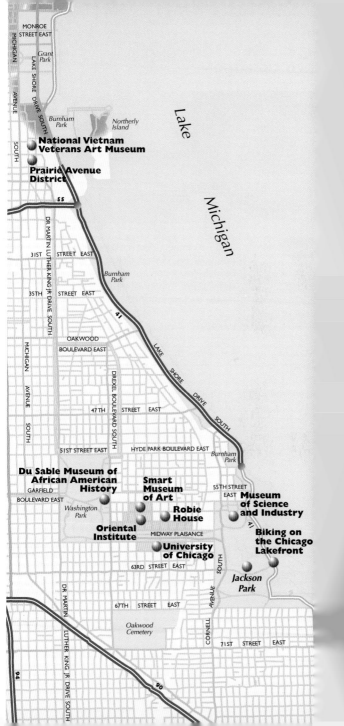

Biking on the Chicago Lakefront

Bike tour and rental shop (left); following the lakefront (right)

THE BASICS

www.chicagobikes.org

Map page 83

Chicago lakefront from Foster Beach on the north to 71st Street on the south

Excellent

Bike Chicago (www.bikechicago.com)

Navy Pier, 600 E. Grand Avenue; Millennium Park, 239 E. Randolph Avenue; Riverwalk, Wacker and Columbus avenues; North Avenue Beach, 1603 N. Lake Shore Drive; Foster Beach, 5200 N. Lake Shore Drive

888/245-3929

$10 per hour, $30 per day for mountain bike or beach cruiser; discounts available if booking online

HIGHLIGHTS

● 18 miles (29km) of paved path
● 31 beaches
● Frequent concession stands in summer
● Views of the skyline
● Bike rentals

Some 18 miles (29km) of paved paths lure walkers, skaters and cyclists to the lakefront, combining exercise and sightseeing. The South Side offers busy routes and wonderful views.

Bike city Chicago is a particularly bike-friendly city, counting over 100 miles (160km) of bike lanes and closing Lake Shore Drive for one day each summer so that cyclists can enjoy the route exclusively. Even the mayor is known to ride around the city streets on a two-wheeler. While the bike lanes on major urban thoroughfares scare the wits from out-of-towners, the lakefront bike path, free of auto traffic, enchants visitors as well as locals. North Side routes are popular and weekend crowds jam the lanes around Oak Street Beach, where cyclists are forced to walk their bikes. For a quieter pedal, point your handlebars south and cruise past the Museum Campus down to the Museum of Science and Industry. The return trip lays out the entire skyline before you in photogenic panoramas as you pedal back. The level terrain is beginner-friendly.

Where to find wheels Bike Chicago offers several seasonal rental stands in Chicago. The best located for southbound trips are at Navy Pier or 63rd Street Beach. The "quadcycle," a four-seater vehicle, only looks fun before you find you are pedaling for the entire family. Bike Chicago also offers city tours by bike each summer, two- to three-hour itineraries devoted to The Lakefront, Neighborhoods or President Obama's Chicago.

African sculpture exhibit (left); exterior of the building (right)

DuSable Museum of African American History

One of Chicago's unsung museums, this one chronicles aspects of black history, chiefly focusing on African-Americans but also encompassing African and Caribbean cultures.

Settlers The museum is named after Chicago's first permanent settler, Jean-Baptiste Point du Sable, a Haitian trader born of a French father and African slave mother in whose home the city's first marriage, election and court decision occurred. Further African-American arrivals came in three main waves—during the late 19th century and during the two world wars—settling mostly on Chicago's South Side. Black businesses became established, while the expanding community provided the voter base for the first blacks to enter Chicago politics. Among the settlers were many musicians, and what became Chicago blues was born—an electrified urban form of rural blues fused with elements of jazz. The turbulent 1960s saw growing radicalism among Chicago's African-Americans, and the beginning of the rise to national prominence of South Side politician Jesse Jackson.

Exhibits The first-floor rooms display items from the permanent collection, including the Harold Washington Wing, which chronicles the triumph of Chicago's first black mayor in 1983. There are also meticulously planned temporary exhibitions, while the Arts and Crafts Festival, displaying original works on African-American themes, is held on the second weekend of July.

THE BASICS

www.dusablemuseum.org
+ Map page 83
✉ 740 E. 56th Place
☎ 773/947-0600
🕐 Tue–Sat 10–5, Sun 12–5
🚇 Red Line: Garfield
🚉 59th Street
🚌 4
♿ Good
✋ Inexpensive; free on Sun

HIGHLIGHTS

● Slavery exhibit, including shackles
● African functional art, including stools and staffs
● Temporary exhibits devoted to black music, art and history
● Craft fair
● Washington Park setting

Hitting a Blues Club

A performer and the audience at Blue Chicago

THE BASICS

Buddy Guy's Legends ▷ 35
B.L.U.E.S ▷ 76
Kingstone Mines ▷ 77
Blue Chicago ▷ 76

HIGHLIGHTS

● Buddy Guy's Legends
● Blue Chicago
● B.L.U.E.S
● Kingston Mines
● Rosa's Lounge

Southern blacks moving north in search of jobs in the 1940s amped up the acoustic blues in Chicago, and hearing the music played live is one of the chief attractions of the city.

Blues background Blues music developed among African slaves working southern plantations and descended from "shout outs" of workers in the fields. By the 1920s it developed its signature musical style of repeated three-cord progressions. Vocalists center the genre, but performers regularly improvise solos above the musical background. Black America's mass exodus from the rural south to the urban north led many musicians to Chicago. The string bands of the Delta region borrowed from jazz groups in the city, amplifying the sound and adding drums, bass, piano and sometimes horns. Innovators Muddy Waters, B.B. King and Buddy Guy established Chicago's electric style, later widely copied by white players like Elvis Presley. The British rock invasion brought the Rolling Stones and Eric Clapton to town to jam with their blues heroes.

A city with the blues Since 1984, on a weekend in early June, marking the opening of summer, the city stages the Chicago Blues Festival, drawing 750,000 listeners to Grant Park. Admission is free and dedicated fest-goers come early with blankets and coolers to stake out their own place on the park lawn. The throng can get fairly boozy by evening, but is all-ages-recommended for most of its duration.

Clarke House exterior
(left); main hall in the
Glessner House (right)

Prairie Avenue District

After the city burned in the Great Fire of 1871, the wealthy and famous moved to the area around Prairie Avenue on the near South Side, where they built elegant mansions, some now open to tours.

From frontier to fancy Hostile Native Americans attacked European settlers in this district in what became known as the Fort Dearborn Massacre in 1812. Only after the Great Fire wiped out the city did builders reconsider the site. The who's who of Chicago society built here, including the Fields (of Field Museum fame), the Pullmans (responsible for luxury Pullman railroad cars) and the Armours (who made a fortune in meat-packing). Later generations would move north and build in the Gold Coast, leaving the Prairie Avenue District to decline. By the mid-20th century many houses were razed, arousing the passions of preservationists who saved most of the 11 remaining Victorian mansions on roughly four blocks.

Two gems Much of the district provides eye candy for passersby, with the exception of two landmarked buildings open for tours.
The oldest, the Greek Revival Clarke House originally owned by hardware dealer Henry B. Clarke, was actually moved to the area from a location farther south.
The more unusual Glessner House is a standout in rugged granite with a fortresslike presence on a corner. The interior is considerably warmer, home to Arts and Crafts furnishings, a central courtyard and custom-made art.

THE BASICS

🔢 F15
✉ 1800 and 1900-blocks of S. Prairie Avenue, 1800-block of S. Indiana, and 211–217 E. Cullerton Street

Glessner House Museum
www.glessnerhouse.org
Organizes guided tours of Clarke House also.
✉ 1800 S. Prairie Avenue
☎ 312/326-1480
🕐 Tours Wed–Sun at 1 and 3 (limit 12 people, first-come first served)

Clarke House Museum
🕐 Tours Wed–Sun at 12, 1 and 2 (limit 12 people, first-come, first-served)
🚇 Green, Orange, Red Lines: Roosevelt
🚌 1, 3, 4
♿ Fair
💲 Moderate; free on Wed

HIGHLIGHTS

● Clarke House
● Glessner House
● Self-guided strolls around the Victorian mansions

Museum of Science and Industry

HIGHLIGHTS

- U-505 submarine
- 1936 *Pioneer Zephyr* train
- The Chick Hatchery
- Miniature fairy castle
- Genetics exhibit
- Apollo 8 Command Module
- Omnimax Theater
- Giant heart

TIP

- Ticket window line-ups are long. To avoid them, order your tickets in advance via the website and have them held at the will-call window.

With 35,000 artifacts spread across 14 acres (5.5ha), this museum easily fills a day. Even know-it-all visitors find hours passing like minutes as they discover new things about the world—and beyond—at every turn.

Flying high The first eye-catching item is a Boeing 727 attached to an interior balcony. Packed with multimedia exhibits, the plane simulates a flight from San Francisco to Chicago, making full use of flaps, rudders and undercarriage, all fully explained. Other flight-related exhibits include a simulated mission aboard a naval F-14 fighter. Reflecting other modes of transportation are the 500mph (804kph) Spirit of America car, a walk-through 1944 German U-boat and the Apollo 8 spacecraft. The moon-circling Apollo craft forms

Clockwise from left: Robot exhibit; Pioneer Zephyr; children looking at a genetics exhibit; the U-505 exhibit—the conning tower; a boy looks through the attack periscope; a demonstration in the control room

just a small part of the excellent Henry Crown Space Center, housed in an adjoining building.

Medical matters A giant heart that will beat to the rhythm of your pulse sits among exhibits detailing the workings of the human body. It's Part of You! The Experience is a multi-faceted exhibit that examines the relationship between the human mind, body and spirit. Play Mindball, a relaxation game; go for a spin on the human hamster wheel; learn how a bionic arm works, and see how your face will age based on your habits and lifestyle.

Industrial issues Addressing industry, MSI re-creates a coal mine, complete with a simulated descent to 600ft (180m) to the coal seam in miners' cars. The Farm exhibit allows you to climb into a John Deere combine harvester and virtually harvest a cornfield.

THE BASICS

www.msichicago.org
🔲 Map page 83
✉ 57th Street at Lake Shore Drive
☎ 773/684-1414
🕐 Mon–Sat 9.30–4, Sun 11–4 (till 5.30 in summer and other dates; see website for times)
🍴 Several cafés
Ⓡ Red Line: Garfield
🚆 55th, 56th, 57th street
🚌 6, 10
♿ Excellent
💵 Moderate; see website for free days schedule; separate charge for Omnimax Theater

More to See

CHINATOWN
www.chicagochinatown.org
The ornate Chinatown Gate arching over Cermak at Wentworth marks the heart of Chinatown. Chicago's oldest Chinese district was founded by 19th-century railroad workers.
🚹 D15 🚇 Red Line: Cermak/Chinatown
🚌 24, 62

JACKSON PARK
In 1893, 27 million people attended the World's Columbian Exposition, in what became Jackson Park, now a green space with sports courts, a Japanese garden and the Museum of Science and Industry (▷ 88).
🚹 Map page 83 ✉ Between S. Stony Island Avenue and Lake Michigan 🚇 Red Line: Garfield 🚈 55th, 56th, 57th streets 🚌 6, 10

JANE ADDAMS HULL-HOUSE MUSEUM
www.uic.edu/jaddams/hull/hull_house.html
In the late 19th century Jane Addams created Hull House, a center in one of the neediest neighborhoods offering English-language and US citizenship courses, child care and other services. A 15-minute slide show tells the story. The rooms of the main building are lined by furnishings and memorabilia.
🚹 C11 ✉ 800 S. Halsted Street
☎ 312/413-5353 🕐 Tue–Fri 10–4, Sun 12–4
🚇 Blue Line: UIC-Halsted 🚈 Halsted
🚌 8 ♿ Fair 🖐 Free

MEXICAN FINE ARTS CENTER MUSEUM
www.nationalmuseumofmexicanart.org
Explore Mexican culture through this collection of 6,000 works by artists of Mexican nationality or descent. Exhibits include prints and drawings, photography, paintings and sculpture.
🚹 Map page 83 ✉ 1852 W. 19th Street
☎ 312/738-1503 🕐 Tue–Sun 10–5 🚇 Pink Line: 18th Street 🚌 50 ♿ Good 🖐 Free

NATIONAL VIETNAM VETERANS ART MUSEUM
www.nvvam.org
Thousands of military dog tags hanging from the lobby's ceiling set the stage for the powerful artwork here. It shows more than 500 pieces by soldiers who

Japanese Gardens in Jackson Park

served in Vietnam as well as some pieces by Iraq war veterans.

🔳 F14 ✉ 1801 S. Indiana Avenue ☎ 312/326-0270 🕐 Tue–Sat 10–5 🚌 1, 3, 4 ✋ Moderate

ORIENTAL INSTITUTE

www.oi.uchicago.edu

The University of Chicago's Oriental Institute is a leading museum and research center specializing in the Middle East. Amid the mummy masks and royal seals, sizeable pieces stand out. Dominating the Egyptian section is a statue of Tutankhamun.

🔳 Map page 83 ✉ 1155 E. 58th Street ☎ 773/702-9514 🕐 Tue, Thu–Sat 10–6, Wed 10–8.30, Sun 12–6 🚇 Red Line: Garfield 🚉 59th Street 🚌 4, 55 ♿ Good ✋ Free (moderate donation)

ROBIE HOUSE

www.wrightplus.org

A famed example of Frank Lloyd Wright's Prairie School style of architecture, built in 1910. The horizontal emphasis reflects the Midwest's open spaces.

🔳 Map page 83 ✉ 5757 S. Woodlawn Avenue ☎ 708/848-1976; tickets 800/514-3849 🕐 Guided tours: times vary, call or see website 🚇 Green Line: Cottage Grove 🚉 59th Street 🚌 4 ♿ Few ✋ Moderate

SMART MUSEUM OF ART

www.smartmuseum.uchicago.edu

With more than 10,000 objects, strong in postwar Chicago art, Japanese painting and contemporary Chinese photography, this museum is a hidden gem.

🔳 Map page 83 ✉ 5550 S. Greenwood Avenue ☎ 773/702-0200 🕐 Tue, Wed, Fri 10–4, Thu 10–8, Sat–Sun 11–5 🚇 Green Line: Garfield 🚌 55 ✋ Free

UNIVERSITY OF CHICAGO

www.uchicago.edu

The oldest buildings on the leafy campus are in English Gothic style, but modernists Eero Saarinen and Ludwig Mies van der Rohe added boxier structures in the 1950s and 60s.

🔳 Map page 83 ✉ Campus is largely bounded by Blackstone Avenue, Cottage Grove, 55th Street and 59th Street 🚇 Green Line: Garfield 🚌 55, 170, 171, 172

Interior of the Smart Museum

A relief on the exterior of the Oriental Institute

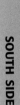

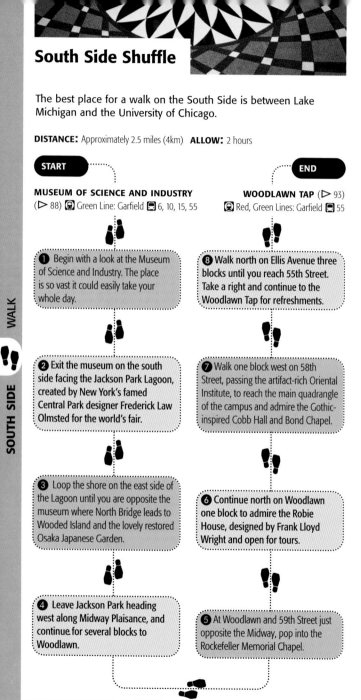

South Side Shuffle

The best place for a walk on the South Side is between Lake Michigan and the University of Chicago.

DISTANCE: Approximately 2.5 miles (4km) **ALLOW:** 2 hours

START

MUSEUM OF SCIENCE AND INDUSTRY
(▷ 88) 🚇 Green Line: Garfield 🚌 6, 10, 15, 55

END

WOODLAWN TAP (▷ 93)
🚇 Red, Green Lines: Garfield 🚌 55

❶ Begin with a look at the Museum of Science and Industry. The place is so vast it could easily take your whole day.

❽ Walk north on Ellis Avenue three blocks until you reach 55th Street. Take a right and continue to the Woodlawn Tap for refreshments.

❷ Exit the museum on the south side facing the Jackson Park Lagoon, created by New York's famed Central Park designer Frederick Law Olmsted for the world's fair.

❼ Walk one block west on 58th Street, passing the artifact-rich Oriental Institute, to reach the main quadrangle of the campus and admire the Gothic-inspired Cobb Hall and Bond Chapel.

❸ Loop the shore on the east side of the Lagoon until you are opposite the museum where North Bridge leads to Wooded Island and the lovely restored Osaka Japanese Garden.

❻ Continue north on Woodlawn one block to admire the Robie House, designed by Frank Lloyd Wright and open for tours.

❹ Leave Jackson Park heading west along Midway Plaisance, and continue for several blocks to Woodlawn.

❺ At Woodlawn and 59th Street just opposite the Midway, pop into the Rockefeller Memorial Chapel.

WALK

SOUTH SIDE

COURT THEATRE
www.courttheatre.org
The University of Chicago's theater has been staging high-quality dramas and musicals for more than 50 years. Noted for its fine acting and innovative staging, the Court deserves the attention more easily snared by downtown and North Side troops.
✉ 5535 W. Ellis Avenue
☎ 773/753-4472
🚇 Green Line: Garfield
🚌 55

DRU'S LOUNGE
Tucked away in Chinatown is this stylish bar-cum-club-cum-eatery, with a well-stocked bar and a hip clientele.
✉ 2101 S. China Place
☎ 312/842-8997 🚇 Red Line: Cermak/Chinatown
🚌 24

HARPO STUDIOS
Oprah Winfrey, America's most popular television talk show host, magazine mogul and celebrity, tapes her self-named show here (Harpo is Oprah spelled backward). While getting tickets is nearly impossible, you can purchase a wide variety of "O" merchandise at her "Oprah Boutique," opened in 2008. To get free tickets to her show, your best bet is to call at least a month in advance, or the day before you want to go.
✚ B9 ✉ 1058 W.

Washington Boulevard
☎ 312/591-9222 🚇 Green Line: UIC/Halsted 🚌 20

OMNIMAX THEATER
www.msichicago.org
A curving, five-story screen embedded with 72 speakers shows large-format IMAX movies on subjects both scientific and entertaining in a separate building attached to the Museum of Science and Industry.
✉ 57th Street and Lake Shore Drive ☎ 773/684-1414
🚇 Green Line: Garfield
🚌 6, 10, 15, 55

REGGIE'S MUSIC JOINT
www.reggieslive.com
Reggie's Music Joint is a bar and grill that also puts on a full range of live music, from punk and indie to home-grown Chicago jazz and blues.

CHINESE NEW YEAR
At the end of January thousands of visitors flock to Chinatown to celebrate Chinese New Year. The parade features dragon dancers, martial artists and Chinese dancers as well as the incongruous bagpipe marching band and assorted politicians. The route runs through the heart of the neighborhood on Wentworth from Cermak to 24th Street. Afterward parade-goers jam the area's many restaurants for dim sum.

There's also a menu of salads, sandwiches, burgers and TV dinners—served just like the TV dinners of old, on a silver foil tray. There are 25 draft beers too, even more by the bottle, and nearby at 2109 S. State is Reggie's Rock Club, if you just want music and no food.
✉ 2105 S. State Street
☎ 312/949-0120 🚇 Red Line: Cermak-Chinatown
🚌 21, 29

VELVET LOUNGE
www.velvetlounge.net
Chicago saxophonist Fred Anderson runs one of the city's most revered jazz listening rooms. The original was destroyed to make way for housing but the club survived the move, with the city's best players on the calendar.
✉ 67 E. Cermak Road
☎ 312/791-9050 🚇 Red Line: Cermak 🚌 21, 29

WOODLAWN TAP
Chicago is famed for its neighborhood taverns, corner taps that serve as places where communities bind. Hyde Park lacks the saloons of other neighborhoods, but the Woodlawn Tap, also known as "Jimmy's," goes a long way to fill in, with three dim rooms filled with brainy academics deep in conversation.
✉ 1172 E. 55th Street
☎ 773/643-5516 🚇 Red, Green Lines: Garfield 🚌 55

Restaurants

CALYPSO CAFÉ ($$)

www.calypsocafechicago
Barack Obama and his family loved the Caribbean food here at this casual café-restaurant in his Hyde Park neighborhood, with dishes like jerk chicken, curried chicken and rice, and Cuban black-bean soup on the excellent menu.
✉ 5211 South Harper Avenue ☎ 773/955-0229 🚇 Metra to 51st/53rd Street 🚌 14, X28

EMPEROR'S CHOICE ($$)

At this small, intimate restaurant, portraits of former Chinese emperors hang above diners who are feasting on some of Chinatown's most creative seafood dishes. For a special occasion order Peking duck a day in advance.
✉ 2238 S. Wentworth Avenue ☎ 312/225-8800 🚇 Red Line: Cermak/Chinatown 🚌 24

GIOCO ($$–$$$)

www.gioco-chicago.com
Fine Tuscan and Umbrian menu combining pizzas, homemade pastas and roast meats served in a former speakeasy.
✉ 1312 S. Wabash Avenue ☎ 312/939-3870 🕓 Closed Sat lunch 🚇 Red, Orange, Green Lines: Roosevelt 🚌 4

OPERA ($$$)

www.opera-chicago.com
With theatrical decor in a former Paramount film warehouse, Opera features upscaled Asian dishes with bold flavors like five-spice squid and Cantonese lobster. Creative cocktails fuel the people-watching in this bustling hot spot
✉ 1301 S. Wabash Avenue ☎ 312/461-0161 🕓 Dinner only 🚇 Red, Orange, Green Lines: Roosevelt 🚌 4

LA PETITE FOLIE ($$$)

www.lapetitefolie.com
A rare, fine-dining outpost in Hyde Park, La Petite Folie serves unfussy French food. It's a popular pre-curtain spot for Court Theatre patrons.
✉ 1504 E. 55th Street ☎ 773/493-1394 🕓 No lunch Sat–Sun; closed Mon 🚇 Green Line: Garfield 🚌 55

PHOENIX ($$)

www.chinatownphoenix.com
This popular Chinatown restaurant serves up panoramic views of the Chicago skyline from picture windows, along with a lively dim sum trade in which servers wheel around small dishes of dumplings, barbecue and meat-filled buns and diners orders. Many of the waiters do not speak English; good humor and the pointing method of ordering prevail. Long waits are common on weekends.
✉ 2131 S. Archer Avenue ☎ 312/328-0848 🚇 Red Line: Cermak 🚌 21, 24

ZAPATISTA ($$$)

www.zapatistacantina.com
Lively Mexican outpost, Zapatista combines regional Mexican dishes such as Oaxacan *moles* and Yucatecan *ceviches* in one eager-to-please menu. The drinks list, too, is comprehensive.
✉ 1307 S. Wabash Avenue ☎ 312/435-1307 🚇 Red, Orange, Green Lines: Roosevelt 🚌 4

CHICAGO'S LITTLE ITALY

Taylor Street was the heart of the immigrant Italian community nearly a century ago. A few old-timers still live in the district but the Italian restaurant scene thrives along a few blocks of Taylor. Rosebud Café (1500 W. Taylor Street) jams fans in for pastas and a convivial atmosphere. Francesca's on Taylor (1400 W. Taylor Street) does homemade pastas in an urban-chic room. The casual Pompei Bakery (1531 W. Taylor Street) serves the best pizza by the slice on the street.

Ironically one of the top tourist sights isn't even in the city. Frank Lloyd Wright's home and original office is in Oak Park. Some 198 neighborhoods aim to lure you, particularly Wicker Park and Bucktown.

Interiors of Stitch (opposite); P45 (left); City Soles (right)

TOP 25

Boutique Browsing in Wicker Park/Bucktown

Roughly 2 miles (3km) due west of the Gold Coast following North Avenue, the scene changes entirely. The urban neighborhood mixes artists, yuppies, immigrants and some of the best shopping and nightlife in the city.

History In the mid-1850s Irish immigrants settled around the Rolling Mill Steel Works. Businesses lined the commercial avenues and residences were tucked in tree-shaded streets behind them. After the Great Fire of 1871 the area boomed as the well-heeled built spacious Victorian mansions. Waves of immigrant Germans, Norwegians, Jews and Poles worked their way through the area following Milwaukee Avenue out of downtown. From the 1930s to the 1970s the area declined. In the 1980s the neighborhoods—Wicker Park to the south and Bucktown adjacent north—took off as trendy nightclubs, restaurants and shops moved in.

Where to shop There is so much choice here. Handmade fashions and accessories by local designers are on show at the boutique Habit (1951 W. Division Street). P45 (1643 N. Damen Avenue) sells cutting-edge women's clothing from emerging American designers, as do neighboring Helen Yi (1645 N. Damen Avenue) with streamlined apparel for women. Pagoda Red (1714 N. Damen Avenue) imports antiques from Asia, from massive Chinese cabinets to fans. Stitch (1723 N. Damen Avenue) is the place for accessories, City Soles (2001 North Avenue) for shoes and Scoop NYC (1702 N. Milwaukee Avenue) for trendy casual clothes.

THE BASICS

www.wickerparkbucktown.com

🗺 Map page 97

✉ The center of the neighborhood is at the three-way intersection of Milwaukee, Damen and North avenues

🕐 Most shops Mon–Sat 11–7, Sun 12–5

🚇 Blue Line: Damen

🚌 50, 70, 72

HIGHLIGHTS

- P45
- Helen Yi
- Habit
- Pagoda Red
- Stitch
- City Soles

FARTHER AFIELD

TOP 25

Frank Lloyd Wright Home and Studio

HIGHLIGHTS

● Barrel vaulted playroom
● Drafting Room with chain harness system to support the roof
● Stained-glass leaded windows
● Skylights
● Wright-designed furniture

TIP

● Advanced tickets are highly recommended. Get them up to midnight the night before the tour from the website or call Etix
☎ 800/514-3849.

The Frank Lloyd Wright Home and Studio provides an insight into the early ideas of one of the greatest and most influential architects of the 20th century. It is an essential stop for anyone interested in design, or in the ability of one man to realize his extraordinary vision.

Organic ideas Working for the Chicago architect Louis Sullivan, the 22-year-old Frank Lloyd Wright designed this home in 1889 for himself, his first wife and their children, and furnished it with pieces he designed. The shingled exterior is not typical of Wright, but the bold geometric shape stands out among the neighboring Queen Anne-style houses. Inside, the open-plan, central fire-places and low ceilings are the earliest examples of the elements that became fundamental in

The exterior of Frank Lloyd Wright's Studio (left); the Children's Playroom inside the house (right)

Wright's so-called Prairie School of Architecture. Particularly notable are the children's playroom, the high-backed chairs in the dining room and the willow tree that grows through the walls in keeping with Wright's theory of organic architecture—architecture in harmony with its surroundings.

Prairie views In 1893, Wright opened his own practice in an annex to the house: A concealed entrance leads into an office showcasing many of Wright's ideas, such as suspended lamps and an open-plan work space. The draftsmen once employed here on seminal Prairie School buildings worked in a stunningly designed room in sight of what was then open prairie. Lloyd Wright's disciples designed 125 buildings here, including the nearby Unity Temple and the Robie House in Hyde Park on Chicago's South Side.

THE BASICS

www.gowright.org
🔁 Map page 96
✉ 951 Chicago Avenue, Oak Park
☎ 708/848-1976
🕐 Guided tours only: Mon–Fri 11.30–3.20; Sat–Sun 11–4 every 20 min
🚇 Green Line: Oak Park Avenue
🚆 Oak Park
🚌 23
♿ Few
💲 Moderate

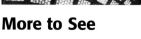

More to See

BALZEKAS MUSEUM OF LITHUANIAN CULTURE

www.balzekasmuseum.org

Regional folk costumes and other Lithuanian historical items form part of an absorbing collection.

➕ Map page 96 ✉ 6500 S. Pulaski Road
☎ 773/582-6500 🕐 Daily 10–4
🚇 Orange Line: Midway 🚌 53A ♿ Few
🖐 Inexpensive

ERNEST HEMINGWAY MUSEUM

www.ehfop.org

A collection remembering the Nobel Prize-winning writer who spent his first 18 years in Oak Park. His birthplace, at 339 N. Oak Park Avenue, is open when the museum is.

➕ Map page 96 ✉ 200 N. Oak Park Avenue
☎ 708/ 848–2222 🕐 Mon–Fri, Sun 1–5, Sat 10–5 🚇 Green Line: Oak Park 🚉 Oak Park
🚌 23 ♿ Few 🖐 Inexpensive

FRANK LLOYD WRIGHT TOUR

www.gowright.org

The Oak Park neighborhood surrounding the architect's home and studio hosts 26 Wright-designed homes, the largest concentration of Wright buildings anywhere in the world. The Wright Foundation rents headsets for self-guided walks past the private homes that last about an hour. Take the tour after visiting the Frank Lloyd Wright Home and Studio (▷ 100), which will familiarize you with the Prairie School style.

✉ Oak Park ☎ 708/848-1976 🚇 Green Line: Oak Park Avenue 🚌 23 ♿ Few
🖐 Moderate

GARFIELD PARK CONSERVATORY

www.garfield-conservatory.org

Providing a refuge from the city, the conservatory has 5 acres (2ha) of tropical and subtropical plants, and is open daily all year round. Highlights include extensive collections of palms, ferns and cacti. Chicagoans come here for expert gardening tips and for shows, when the opening hours are extended.

➕ Map page 96 ✉ 300 N. Central Park Avenue ☎ 312/746-5100 🕐 Sun–Tue, Thu–Sat 9–5, Wed 9–8 🚇 Green Line: Conservatory-Central Park 🚌 82 ♿ Few
🖐 Free

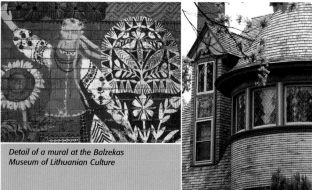

Detail of a mural at the Balzekas Museum of Lithuanian Culture

Walter H. Gale's House, designed by Frank Lloyd Wright

Shopping

THE ALLEY

www.thealley.com

If your idea of an accessory is a Zippo lighter or a Che Guevara belt buckle, the Alley stores, a group of alternative clothing stockists, are just the place to find it, plus leather jackets and motorcycle boots.

✉ 3228 N. Clark Street
☎ 773/883-1800
Ⓡ Brown, Red Lines: Belmont
🚌 22, 36

BEATNIX

Packed from floor to ceiling, this stash of wild and unbelievable attire is like Disneyland for the daring.

✉ 3400 N. Halsted Avenue
☎ 773/281-6933 Ⓡ Brown, Red Lines: Belmont 🚌 152

BELMONT ARMY SURPLUS

www.belmontarmy.com

This former army surplus store has expanded over three floors to become a top Chicago spot for hiking boots, backpacks and more.

✉ 855 W. Belmont Avenue
☎ 773/549-1038 Ⓡ Brown, Red Lines: Belmont 🚌 77

BETA BOUTIQUE

www.betaboutique.com

Bag a fashion bargain at Chicago's only permanent sample-sale store that features designer samples and overstock items from most of the top labels at discount prices.

✉ 2016 W Concord Place
☎ 773/276-0905 Ⓒ Closed

Mon–Wed Ⓑ Blue Line: Damen 🚌 50, 56, 72

BROADWAY ANTIQUES MARKET

www.bamchicago.com

The 75-plus dealers at this two-floor antiques haven sell everything from art deco to mid-20th-century modern.

✉ 6130 N. Broadway Avenue
☎ 773/743-5444 Ⓡ Red Line: Granville 🚌 136

DSW SHOE WAREHOUSE

www.dswshoe.com

Whether in need of designer shoes for a top night out or simply solid footwear, this long-established outlet is the place to find them.

✉ 3131 N. Clark Street
☎ 773/975-7182 Ⓡ Brown, Red Lines: Belmont 🚌 77

THREADLESS KIDS

www.kids.threadless.com

Cute, clever and creative,

CURIOUS CLOTHES

Should the sensible buying of sensible clothes for sensible everyday wear suddenly become a stultifyingly dull pursuit, you can let your sartorial imaginations run riot at Chicago Costume Company (✉ 1120 W. Fullerton Parkway). This enormous store carries hundreds of outrageous costumes, masks and assorted outlandish accessories for sale or rent, for the dresser who dares.

the graphic designs on these screenprinted T-shirts and hoodies for children and babies were such a big hit with parents that they now stock adult sizes, too.

✉ 1905 W. Division Street
☎ 773/698-7042 Ⓑ Blue Line: Division 🚌 9, 70

UNABRIDGED BOOKSTORE

www.unabridgedbookstore.com

Chicago's leading gay bookstore and a rare independent bookseller offers reads on a wide array of topics. Well-read employees offer their personal touts for books they like in notes attached to the racks.

✉ 3251 N. Broadway
☎ 773/883-9119 Ⓡ Red Line: Belmont 🚌 36, 77

UNCLE FUN

www.unclefunchicago.com

All ages from elementary schoolkids to their parents love to browse Uncle Fun, crammed with vintage metal wind-up toys, cast-off stickers, cheap plastic animals, gag gifts and trinkets. Uncle Fun's owners also run the stationery shop Paper Boy across the street with considerably more serious, artistically inclined cards, gift wrap and pens.

✉ 1338 W. Belmont Street
☎ 773/477-8223 Ⓡ Brown Line: Paulina 🚌 77

Entertainment and Nightlife

BEAT KITCHEN
www.beatkitchen.com
Smallish venue that makes a good setting for folk and rock acts, predominantly from around Chicago.
✉ 2100 W. Belmont Avenue ☎ 773/281-4444 🚇 Brown, Red Lines: Belmont 🚌 22

CHICAGO CENTER FOR THE PERFORMING ARTS
www.theaterland.com
An expanding and well-equipped performance art and education complex, which stages diverse drama and music in its 340-seat main hall, as well as various other events.
✉ 777 N. Green Street ☎ 312/733-6000 🚇 Blue Line: Chicago 🚌 8, 66

CUBBY BEAR LOUNGE
www.cubbybear.com
Its location opposite Wrigley Field makes this sports bar a favorite spot for post-Cub games. The live music spans rock, country, reggae and blues, plus dancing and beer.
✉ 1059 W. Addison Street ☎ 773/327-1662 🚇 Brown Line: Addison 🚌 22, 152

ELBO ROOM
www.elboroomchicago.com
This innovative venue features live alternative rock, poetry readings and comedy.
✉ 2871 N. Lincoln Avenue ☎ 773/549-5549 🚇 Brown Line: Diversey 🚌 11

GREEN MILL COCKTAIL LOUNGE
www.greenmilljazz.com
Classic Uptown jazz club that dates back to Chicago's Prohibition Days as a speakeasy. Home of the Sunday night Uptown Poetry Slam, an open-mike night for performance poets that has spawned imitators the world over.
✉ 4802 N. Broadway Avenue ☎ 773/878-5552 🚇 Red Line: Lawrence 🚌 36

METRO
www.metrochicago.com
Major mid-size venue for live rock, with ample space for dancing and plentiful seating with good views. Other levels have a nightclub and coffee bar.
✉ 3730 N. Clark Street ☎ 773/549-0203 🚇 Brown Line: Addison 🚌 22, 152

RAVINIA FESTIVAL
From mid-June to Labor Day, the northern suburb of Highland Park plays host to the Ravinia Festival. The summer home of the Chicago Symphony Orchestra, Ravinia also stages rock and jazz concerts, dance events and other cultural activities. Chartered buses ferry festival goers the 25 miles (40km) from central Chicago; you can also get there by commuter train. Details ☎ 847/433-8819; www.ravinia.org.

MUSIC BOX THEATRE
www.musicboxtheatre.com
Independent, classic and foreign films fill the slate at this 1929 Lakeview movie palace with twinkling stars in the ceiling and an organ employed during Christmas holiday sing-alongs.
✉ 3733 N. Southport Avenue ☎ 773/871-6604 🚇 Brown Line: Southport 🚌 9, 77, 80

OLD TOWN SCHOOL OF FOLK MUSIC
www.oldtownschool.org
Set in "restaurant row" of the Lincoln Square neighborhood, this folk and world music venue hosts concerts in an intimate setting. The school also offers lessons in everything from ukelele to Qi Gong exercise.
✉ 4544 N. Lincoln Avenue ☎ 773/728-6000 🚇 Brown Line: Western 🚌 11, 49

SHEFFIELD'S WINE & BEER
www.sheffieldchicago.com
On a sunny day, head for the patio bar to try the microbrews, mostly made on the premises.
✉ 3258 N. Sheffield Avenue ☎ 773/281-4989 🚇 Brown, Red Lines: Belmont 🚌 9, 77

THE WILD HARE
www.wildharemusic.com
Top-notch live reggae and other Caribbean and African sounds in the heart of Wrigleyville.
✉ 3530 N. Clark Street ☎ 773/327-4273 🚇 Brown Line: Addison 🚌 22, 152

Restaurants

PRICES

Prices are approximate, based on a 3-course meal for one person.

$$$$	over $50
$$$	$31–$50
$$	$16–$30
$	up to $15

ARUN'S ($$$$)

www.arunsthai.com
Superb Thai fare, with subtle spicing reflecting the exceptional talent in the kitchen. Tasting menus only.
✉ 4156 N. Kedzie Avenue
☎ 773/539-1909 ⦿ Dinner only; closed Mon ⦿ Brown Line: Kedzie ⦿ 80, 82

BARBAKAN RESTAURANT ($)

www.barbakanrestaurant.com
Unprepossessing interior, complete with aging formica tables, conceals delicious Polish food at low prices; the soup options change daily.
✉ 3145 N. Central Avenue
☎ 773/202-8181 ⦿ Blue Line: Belmont ⦿ 85

BISTRO CAMPAGNE ($$$)

www.bistrocampagne.com
Intimate setting for quality French cuisine from a small but well-chosen menu; come early in the week to avoid the crowds. Outdoor dining in summer in a pleasant garden.
✉ 4518 N. Lincoln Avenue
☎ 773/271-6100 ⦿ Dinner only; Sun brunch ⦿ Brown Line: Western ⦿ 11, 49, 78

CAFÉ LURA ($)

Live music and cabaret provide reason to call here in the evenings, but stop in earlier in the day for the Polish fare.
✉ 3184 N. Milwaukee Avenue
☎ 773/736-3033 ⦿ Blue Line: Belmont ⦿ 56, 77

CHICAGO BRAUHAUS ($$–$$$)

www.chicagobrauhaus.com
Chicago has lost many of its famed German restaurants. The 40-plus-year-old Brauhaus proudly waves the flag with a menu of plentiful standards like schnitzel and sausage and frothy beers on tap. The house oompah band gets dancers to their feet.
✉ 4732 N. Lincoln Avenue
☎ 773/784-4444 ⦿ No lunch Sat; closed Tue ⦿ Brown Line: Western ⦿ 11, 4

INDIA IN CHICAGO

Chicago's Indian community thrives along Devon Avenue on the far North Side of the city. Bollywood video stores and sari shops occasionally intersperse the long string of restaurants that line either side of the street west of Western Avenue. Top choices include Indian Garden (✉ 2546 W. Devon Avenue ☎ 312/280-4910) and Tiffin (✉ 2536 W. Devon Avenue ☎ 773/338-2143). Many places feature a bargain-price buffet for the midday meal.

CLUB LUCKY ($–$$)

www.clubluckychicago.com
The Italian menu is long at this lively neighborhood supper club in Bucktown, though the food takes second place to the socializing.
➕ A4 ✉ 1824 W. Wabansia Street ☎ 773/227-2308
⦿ Dinner only weekends
⦿ Blue Line: Damon
⦿ 7

MIA FRANCESCA ($$)

www.miafrancesca.com
There is always a wait at this favorite of Chicago natives. Expect excellent seafood specials and wonderful red-sauced fare, but it's the pasta in large amounts and top-notch pizza that make this undersized eatery one of Lake View's most popular haunts.
✉ 3311 N. Clark Street
☎ 773/281-3310 ⦿ No lunch Mon–Fri ⦿ Brown, Red, Purple Lines: Belmont ⦿ 22, 77

SPRING ($$$–$$$$)

www.springrestaurant.net
A downtown-caliber restaurant in Wicker Park, Spring specializes in Asian-inflected seafood dishes prepared with high-quality ingredients and plated elegantly. The semi-underground digs were once a Russian bathhouse bearing the original glazed white tiles.
✉ 2039 W. North Avenue
☎ 773/395-7100 ⦿ Dinner only. Closed Mon ⦿ Blue Line: Damen ⦿ 50, 72

Chicago's hotels are largely clustered downtown within walking distance of shopping, restaurants, nightlife and museums. Around O'Hare Airport are lodgings that cater primarily to business travelers.

Introduction

Chicago's hotels concentrate in the tourist regions downtown. But within that region, where you stay depends very much on what you aim to do.

An Experience
If it's shopping you seek, look for something on the near North Side or along the Magnificent Mile. Loop district hotels plant you closest to many top cultural attractions, including the Art Institute of Chicago and Randolph Street theaters. River North hotels provide great access to restaurants and nightlife. To experience life as a Chicago resident you might try something in close proximity to Wrigley Field or the Lincoln Park Zoo.

For Your Own Budget
Most of the city's luxury hotels, including the Trump Tower, Park Hyatt and Peninsula, are on or near the Magnificent Mile, offering easy access to high-end shops. Mid-range hotels are scattered throughout the Loop, River North and near North Side regions. Budget hotels tend to be pushed to the margins of downtown or in North Side neighborhoods such as Lakeview.

Best Times to Visit
Because business travel traffic is so vital to hoteliers, many of them drop their rates to lure in weekend guests. You probably won't find such bargains in the height of summer, but during the off-season the sales can be dramatic.

DATES TO AVOID
Chicago has the biggest convention center in the country, McCormick Place. Some conventions swell to take every hotel room in the region. Others, such as the National Restaurant Show each May, make getting a restaurant reservation difficult. Business travelers account for 55 percent of hotel business downtown. September, October, November and May are big convention months. If crowds concern you, phone ahead when booking your hotel and ask about group business during your stay.

Budget Hotels

BEST WESTERN HAWTHORNE TERRACE

www.hawthorneterrace.com
Wrigley Field is a short walk from this 59-room neighborhood inn with nice-for-the-price amenities including Wi-Fi and a fitness center. Also close to Wrigleyville and North Halsted restaurant scene, as well as the Lincoln Park lakefront.
🔁 Off map at C1 ✉ 3434 N. Broadway ☎ 888/860-3400; fax 773/244-3435 🔘 Red Line: Addison 🚌 36

CITY SUITES HOTEL

www.cityinns.com
Most of the 45 rooms are suites—and good value. But it's a shame about the lively, and rather loud shopping and nightlife strip on the doorstep.
🔁 Off map at C1 ✉ 933 W. Belmont Avenue ☎ 773/404-3400 or 800/248-9108 🔘 Brown, Red Lines: Belmont 🚌 77

DAYS INN CHICAGO— LINCOLN PARK

www.daysinn.com
Near the lakefront but 3 miles (5km) north of the Loop is this simple but decent hotel. It's on a busy intersection, and surrounded by restaurants and shopping, but train and bus stops are close

by and free continental breakfast is included.
🔁 Off map ✉ 644 W. Diversey ☎ 773/525-7010 🔘 Red Line: Fullerton and Wellington 🚌 22, 76

HOSTEL CHICAGO INTERNATIONAL

www.hichicago.org
Also known as the J. Ira & Nicki Harris Family Hostel, this 1886 building on the southern edge of the Loop offers 500 comfortable beds in immaculate if spartan dorms that provide a perfect low-budget stay. Guests qualify for free breakfast and a range of discounts on local tours and attractions.
🔁 F11 ✉ 24 E. Congress Parkway ☎ 312/360-0300 🔘 Red Line: Harrison 🚌 6, 146

OHIO HOUSE

www.ohiohousemotel.com
This dependable, simple motel has 50 rooms and

offers exceptionally good rates in a River North location. Free parking and Wi-Fi.
🔁 E8 ✉ 600 N. La Salle Street ☎ 312/943-6000; fax 312/943-6063 🔘 Red Line: Grand 🚌 37, 41

RED ROOF INN CHICAGO DOWNTOWN

www.redroof-chicago-downtown.com
Rooms are small but well planned in a historic building, some with mini-refrigerator and microwave. The location can't be beat at this price, two blocks off Michigan Avenue in the bustling and usually high-price Streetersville district.
🔁 F8 ✉ 162 E. Ontario Street ☎ 312/787-3580; fax 312/787-1299 🔘 Red Line: Grand 🚌 65, 157

WILLOWS HOTEL

www.cityinns.com/willows
A hotel with 55 great-value rooms on a residential street in Lake View, close to the lake, Lincoln Park and numerous bars and restaurants. The building dates from the 1920s and is full of character—the lobby is especially charming, with a fireplace and high windows.
🔁 Off map at D1 ✉ 555 W. Surf Street ☎ 773/528-8400 or 800/787-3108 🔘 Brown Line: Diversey 🚌 36

Mid-Range Hotels

PRICES

Expect to pay between $150 and $250 for a mid-range hotel.

AFFINIA CHICAGO

www.affinia.com
The boutique Affinia has a touch of retro-chic about its 215 spacious guest rooms and suites, while its rooftop C-View cocktail bar gives great views. The C-House restaurant is also highly rated; the location could not be better: a block from the Magnificent Mile.
⊞ F7 ⊠ 166 E. Superior ☎ 312/787-6000; fax 312/787-4331 🚇 Red Line: Chicago 🚌 66, 151

AMALFI HOTEL

www.amalfihotelchicago.com
Near downtown and the Magnificent Mile, this new Italian-style boutique hotel serves a complimentary breakfast on every floor, and nightly hors d'oeuvres.
⊞ E9 ⊠ 20 W. Kinzie Street ☎ 312/395-9000 or 877/262-5341; fax 312/395-9001 🚇 Red Line: Grand 🚌 22

BURNHAM

www.burnhamhotel.com
Creative use of the historic Reliance Building has yielded 141 comfortable, smallish rooms with some period details.
⊞ E10 ⊠ 1 W. Washington Street ☎ 312/782-1111 or 877/294-9712; fax 312/782-0899 🚇 Blue, Red Lines: Washington 🚌 147, 151

COURTYARD BY MARRIOTT

www.marriott.com
The 337 comfortable, large rooms are designed for business travelers. The Loop is adjacent.
⊞ F8 ⊠ 30 E. Hubbard Street ☎ 312/329-2500; fax 312/329-0293 🚇 Red Line: Grand 🚌 36

EMBASSY SUITES

www.embassysuiteschicago.com
The 367 suites are in a good location for Michigan Avenue shopping and River North nightlife. Substantial buffet breakfast and a free evening cocktail party included.
⊞ E8 ⊠ 600 N. State Street ☎ 312/943-3800; fax 312/943-7629 🚇 Red Line: Grand 🚌 36

HILTON CHICAGO

www.chicagohilton.com
More than 1,500 rooms,

BOOKING

Rooms can be reserved by phone, online, fax or mail; book as early as possible. A deposit (usually by credit card) equivalent to the nightly rate will ensure your room is held at least until 6pm; inform the hotel if you are arriving later. Credit card is the usual payment method; traveler's checks or cash can be used, but payment might then be expected in advance. The total charge will include the city's 15.4 percent sales and room tax.

a pervasive sense of grandeur and the city's largest hotel health club.
⊞ F13 ⊠ 720 S. Michigan Avenue ☎ 312/922-4400 🚇 Red Line: Harrison 🚌 1, 3, 4, 6, 146

HOMEWOOD SUITES BY HILTON

www.homewoodsuites chicago.com
These comfortable apartment rooms are some of the best value in town; breakfast included, free Wi-Fi, business center access, a pool and fitness center, and complimentary snacks and drinks four nights a week. Many rooms have grand views of the Wrigley Building.
⊞ F7 ⊠ 40 East Grand Avenue ☎ 312/644-2222; fax 312/644-7777 🚇 Red Line: Chicago 🚌 29, 36

HOTEL ALLEGRO

www.allegrochicago.com
This well-established Loop hotel, known for its whimsical yet luxurious decor, has undergone a major renovation.
⊞ E9 ⊠ 171 W. Randolph Street ☎ 800/643-1500 or 312/236-0123; fax 312/236-0917 🚇 Brown, Orange Lines: Randolph/Wells 🚌 37

HOTEL INDIGO CHICAGO

www.goldcoastchicagohotel.com
A new boutique hotel in an older building on a Gold Coast residential street close to the Magnificent Mile.
⊞ E5 ⊠ 1244 N. Dearborn Parkway ☎ 312/787-4980;

fax 312/787-4069 Red Line: Clark/Division 37, 156

HOTEL MONACO

www.monaco-chicago.com
Stylish striped wallpaper and offbeat colors provide zip to this 192-room boutique hotel in the Loop. Request a room with a window seat to enjoy the view. Free Wi-Fi and a complimentary wine reception nightly.
F9 225 N. Wabash Avenue 866/610-0081; fax 312/960-1883 Brown, Green, Orange Lines: State, Lake 29

HOTEL SAX CHICAGO

www.hotelsaxchicago.com
The lobby, bar and all 353 guest rooms of this former House of Blues Hotel were remodeled in 2007. While the rooms are stylish, most visitors stay here because it's adjacent to six restaurants, an upscale "bowling lounge," the Crunch gym, and the House of Blues restaurant and club.
E9 333 N. Dearborn 312/245-0333 or 877/569-3742 Red Line: Grand 22

MILLENNIUM KNICKER-BOCKER HOTEL

www.millenniumhotels.com
First built in 1927, its Martini Bar and Crystal Ballroom retain a feel for that era. A multimillion-dollar make-over has brought its 305 rooms up to 21st-century standards.
F6 163 East Walton

Place 312/751-8100; fax 312/751-9205 Red Line: Chicago 145, 146, 147, 151

OLD TOWN CHICAGO BED & BREAKFAST

www.oldtownchicago.com
Four suites, sumptuously furnished in a manner befitting the retro art deco style of this town house. In a peaceful residential street in the Old Town.
D5 1442 N. North Park Avenue 312/440-9268 Brown Line: Sedgwick 72

RENAISSANCE CHICAGO

www.marriott.com
A convenient Loop location and 553 spacious, well-equipped rooms make this a good choice.
E9 1 W. Wacker Drive 800/468-3571 or 312/372-7200; fax 312/372-0093 Red Line: Lake, State;

Brown, Green Lines: State 2, 10, 11, 44

SOFITEL CHICAGO WATER TOWER

www.sofitel.com
Striking glass hotel from French hoteliers Sofitel with good views of the John Hancock and a smart Mag Mile locale. Modern but comfortable furnishings in the rooms.
F7 20 E. Chestnut Street 312/324-4000; fax 312/324-4026 Red Line: Chicago 22, 66

SUTTON PLACE

www.chicago.suttonplace.com
In a strikingly modern exterior amid Gold Coast brownstones, with 246 comfortable rooms.
F6 21 Bellevue Place 312/266-2100 or 866/378-8866; fax 312/266-2103 Red Line: Clarke, Division North Michigan Avenue bus

TREMONT HOTEL

www.tremontchicago.com
This elegant, 130-room, Tudor-style hotel is a stone's throw from Michigan Avenue.
F7 100 E. Chestnut Street 312/751-1900; fax 312/751-8691 Red Line: Chicago 145, 146, 147, 151

THE WHITEHALL

www.thewhitehallhotel.com
First opened in the 1920s, this 222-room hotel now has English-style furniture and modern amenities.
F7 105 E. Delaware Place 866/753-4081 or 312/944-6300 Red Line: Chicago 145, 146, 147, 151

Luxury Hotels

PRICES

Expect to pay between $250 and $650 or more for a luxury hotel.

THE DRAKE

www.thedrakehotel.com
Modeled on an Italian Renaissance palace. Some of the 535 rooms have lake views.

✚ F6 ⊠ 140 E. Walton Place ☎ 800/553-7253 or 312/787-2200 🚇 Red Line: Chicago 🚌 145, 146, 147, 151

FAIRMONT HOTEL

www.fairmont.com/chicago
Winning views over Grant Park, the city and the lake; the 692 rooms are comfortable and tasteful. Use of health club.

✚ F9 ⊠ 200 N. Columbus Drive ☎ 866/540-4408 or 312/565-8000 🚇 Brown, Orange Lines: State, Lake 🚌 4

INTERCONTINENTAL CHICAGO

www.icchicagohotel.com
A lavish men's club built in 1929 now houses this hotel. The mosaic-tile indoor pool is a must-see. The 790 rooms are split between the historic building and a modern tower.

✚ F8 ⊠ 505 N. Michigan Avenue ☎ 312/944--4100; fax 312/944-1320 🚇 Red Line: Grand 🚌 143, 144, 145, 146, 151

PALMER HOUSE HILTON

www.hilton.com
This is not just a luxurious hotel but a historic and architectural landmark, the Palmer House has been in business since 1871 and is the oldest still-operating hotel in the USA.

✚ F10 ⊠ 17 East Monroe Street ☎ 312/726-7500; fax 312/917-1707 🚌 145, 146, 147, 151

PARK HYATT CHICAGO

www.parkchicago.hyatt.com
The best rooms, and the hotel's highly regarded NoMI restaurant, peer directly over the historic Water Tower. Photography and fine art complement the modern interiors.

✚ F7 ⊠ 800 N. Michigan Avenue ☎ 312/335-1234; fax 312/239-4000 🚇 Red Line: Chicago 🚌 66, 143, 144, 145, 146, 151

THE PENINSULA CHICAGO

www.chicago.peninsula.com
A gilded link in the Asia-based chain, the Peninsula Chicago pampers guests with top-floor lap pool with skyline views and room controls for temperature, curtains and valet notices from a bedside console.

✚ F7 ⊠ 108 E. Superior Street ☎ 866/288-8889 or 312/337-2888; fax 312/751-2888 🚇 Red Line: Chicago 🚌 143, 144, 145, 146, 151

RITZ-CARLTON CHICAGO

www.fourseasons.com/chicagorc
Whim-catering hotel popular with celebrities passing through. The restaurant is a stand out. Shoppers like the locale just off Michigan Avenue at Water Tower Place.

✚ F7 ⊠ 160 E. Pearson Street ☎ 800/621-6906 or 312/266-1000; fax 312/266-1194 🚇 Red Line: Chicago 🚌 143, 144, 145, 146, 151

LUXE LURES

Chicago's best hotels are, of course, the most expensive. But budget-conscious travelers can still enjoy the settings there. Several, including the Ritz-Carlton, Four Seasons and the Peninsula, serve afternoon tea (around $20 per person). Both the Peninsula and the Park Hyatt Chicago operate sophisticated bars that draw local swells as well as guests. The top-floor spa at the Peninsula is a splurge, but gives access to a lap pool with skyline views.

TRUMP INTERNATIONAL HOTEL & TOWER

www.trumpchicago.com
The 92-story Trump oozes both luxury and an understated elegance, from its spacious guest rooms to its marble lobby and zebrawood elevators. Pool, superb spa, the intimate Sixteen restaurant, and the buzzing Rebar cocktail bar with dazzling night-time views over the river.

✚ F8 ⊠ 410 N. Wabash Avenue ☎ 312/644-0900 🚇 Red Line: Grand 🚌 29, 143, 144, 145, 146, 151

Use this section to familiarize yourself with travel to and within Chicago. Planning can help save money: The multiday visitor's pass allowing unlimited trips on the mass transit system is sold in advance.

Planning Ahead

When To Go

June, July and August are the busiest months, but the weather can be tryingly hot. May, September and October are better months to visit, with fewer crowds and warm but less extreme weather. Events and festivals take place year-round. Major conventions in May, September, October and November cause hotel space to be scarce.

TIME

Chicago is one hour behind New York, two hours ahead of Los Angeles and six hours behind the UK.

AVERAGE DAILY MAXIMUM TEMPERATURES											
JAN	FEB	MAR	APR	MAY	JUN	JUL	AUG	SEP	OCT	NOV	DEC
22°F	26°F	37°F	49°F	59°F	69°F	74°F	72°F	65°F	53°F	40°F	27°F
-6°C	-3°C	3°C	9°C	15°C	21°C	23°C	22°C	18°C	12°C	4°C	-3°C

Spring (mid-March to May) Very changeable; sometimes snow, sometimes sun, but generally mild.

Summer (June to mid-September) Varies from warm to very hot, sometimes uncomfortably so with high humidity.

Autumn (mid-September to October) Though changeable, it is often mild with sunny days.

Winter (November to mid-March) Often very cold with heavy snow and strong winds. Winds can be strong any time and particularly cold when, usually in winter, they come from the north.

WHAT'S ON

January/February *Chinese New Year*: In Chinatown.

March *St. Patrick's Day*: The city turns green, and there's a parade through the Loop.

April *Baseball season* opens. *Chicago Antiques and Fine Art Fair*.

May *Polish Constitution Day* (first Sat): Chicago's Polish Americans celebrate with a parade and events focusing on Polish culture.

Wright Plus: See inside Oak Park homes designed by Frank Lloyd Wright.

June *Chicago Blues Festival*: Local and international artists perform in Grant Park.

Printer's Row Book Fair: Used-book shops host events.

Chicago Gospel Festival: Gospel music in Millennium Park.

July *Taste of Chicago*: feeding frenzy; 11 days leading up to July 4, thousands sample dishes from city restaurants.

Independence Day (Jul 4): Special events such as fireworks displays, the largest taking place in Grant Park.

August *Ravinia Festival* (mid-June to Labor Day): Two months of the Chicago Symphony Orchestra, pop, folk and rock music, with picnicking on the lawns.

Chicago Air & Water Show: Spectacular stunts performed along the lakefront.

September *Chicago Jazz Festival*: Jazz stars headline free concerts in Grant Park.

October *Chicago Marathon*.

November/December *Festival of Lights*: Lights along the Magnificent Mile.

Chicago Online

www.egov.cityofchicago.org
The city government website. Chicagoans use this to pay their bills and make complaints, but it holds plenty of interest to visitors.

www.choosechicago.com
Part of the above, but aimed more squarely at visitors.

www.gochicago.com
Official site for international visitors.

www.chicagotribune.com
The online version of Chicago's biggest-circulation daily newspaper.

www.suntimes.com
The online version of Chicago's tabloid daily newspaper, with full access to news and feature stories, plus sports and, if you should want it, access to its advertisements.

www.chicagoreader.com
The website of the city's long-established alternative weekly newspaper, the *Chicago Reader*, with a different slant on city affairs and its own recommendations for entertainment.

www.chicago.metromix.com
Chicago edition of a national site providing informative listings, covering events, museums, dining, nightlife and more.

www.urchicago.com
Opinionated takes on the Chicago clubbing scene and much more about the city from a late-night perspective.

www.timeoutchicago.com
A glossy, edgy magazine with listings, trend pieces and feature stories on special events.

PRIME TRAVEL SITES

www.fodors.com
A complete travel-planning site. Research prices and the weather; reserve air tickets, cars and rooms; ask questions (and get answers) from fellow visitors; and find links to other sites.

www.transitchicago.com
The website of the Chicago Transit Authority explains all there is to know about using the city's buses and El trains, the fares and ticket types, with route maps that can be downloaded and lots more.

INTERNET ACCESS

Harold Washington Library Center
www.chipublib.org
The main city center branch of the Chicago Public Library has internet access available to visitors with photo ID.
➕ E11 ✉ 400 S. State Street ☎ 312/747-4300
🕐 Mon–Thu 9–9, Fri–Sat 9–5, Sun 1-5 💲 Free

Screenz Digital Universe
www.screenz.com
Broadband connections and screened-off workstations with all the appropriate software.
➕ C1 ✉ 2717 N. Clark Street ☎ 773/348-9300
🕐 Mon–Fri 8am–midnight, Sat–Sun 9am–midnight
💲 $10–$12 per hour

Getting There

ENTRY REQUIREMENTS

Visitors to Chicago from outside the US require a machine-readable passport, valid for at least six months. Passports issued on or after October 26, 2004 must include a biometric identifier; UK passports already issued will still qualify for up to 90 days visa-free travel in the visa-waiver scheme. Visitors using the visa-waiver program must register their details online before traveling. Check the current situation before you leave (US Embassy visa information ☎ 202/643-4000; www.usembassy.gov; British Embassy in the US www.britainusa.com). Be sure to leave plenty of time to clear security as the levels of checks are constantly being stepped up.

AIRPORTS

Chicago's O'Hare International Airport is 17 miles (27km) northwest of the Loop and takes all international flights and most domestic flights. Midway Airport, 8 miles (13km) southwest of the Loop, is a quieter alternative for domestic flights.

FROM O'HARE INTERNATIONAL AIRPORT

For information on O'Hare International Airport ☎ 773/686-3700; www.ohare.com.
Continental Airport Express (☎ 773/247-1200; www.airportexpress.com) runs minibuses between O'Hare and the Loop every 10–15 minutes 6am–11.30pm (fare $27; journey time 60 minutes). Pick them up from outside the arrivals terminal. Make a reservation for the trip from your hotel to the airport.

Chicago Transit Authority (☎ 888/968-7282; www.transitchicago.com) operates Blue Line trains between O'Hare and the Loop (24 hours; journey time 45 minutes; fare $2.25). Follow the signs from the arrivals hall to the station. However, it is safer to take a taxi late at night from either airport. Taxis wait outside the arrivals terminal and the fare to the Loop or nearby hotels is about $35–$40.

ARRIVING AT MIDWAY AIRPORT

For information about Midway Airport ☎ 773/838-0600; www.ohare.com.
Continental Airport Express runs minibuses

to the Loop every 15 minutes 6am–10.30pm (fare around $22; journey time 60 minutes). Pick the minibus up from outside Door 3 on the lower level.

Chicago Transit Authority runs Orange Line trains to the Loop 5am–11.30pm (fare $2,25; journey time 30 minutes). Taxis wait at the arrivals terminal. The fare to the Loop or nearby hotels is approximately $35.

ARRIVING BY BUS

Greyhound buses (☎ 800/231-2222; 312/408-5821; www.greyhound.com) arrive at 630 W. Harrison Street, six blocks southwest of the Loop. MegaBus (www.megabus.com), which serves eight Midwestern states with budget-priced fares, stops at Union Station on the east side of S. Canal Street, between Jackson Boulevard and Adams Street.

ARRIVING BY CAR

Chicago has good Interstate access: I-80 and I-90 are the major east–west routes; I-55 and I-57 arrive from the south. I-94 runs through the city linking the north and south suburbs. To reach the Loop from O'Hare airport use I-90/94. From Midway airport take I-55, linking with the northbound I-90/94 for the Loop. Journeys take from 45 to 90 minutes and 30 to 60 minutes respectively depending on traffic and weather. Try to avoid rush hours, 7–9am and 4–7pm.

There are more than half a dozen auto rental agencies at both O'Hare and Midway. Rates usually start in the range of $70 to $100 per day, $150 to $200 per week, with fuel as an extra charge.

ARRIVING BY TRAIN

Amtrak trains (Information ☎ 800/872-7245 or 312/655-2385; www.amtrak.com) use Chicago's Union Station, junction of W. Adams and S. Canal streets.

CHICAGO GREETER

The Chicago Office of Tourism's Department of Cultural Affairs runs a program to match volunteer residents with inquiring visitors. Chicago Greeters won't meet you at the airport, nor even on the day that you arrive, but by prior arrangement will spend two to four hours showing you around the city and providing an insider's point of view. The service is free but requires a seven-day advance registration via the website www.chicagogreeter.com. Greeters will escort one to six visitors on the itinerary of their choice ranging from outings themed to food or history or itineraries that look at a specific neighborhood.

Getting Around

DRIVING IN CHICAGO

Driving in the city is stressful: Use public transportation. Many hotels have parking lots, otherwise overnight parking is difficult and very costly. During the day, street parking is often limited to two hours; spaces in the Loop are near impossible to find.

VISITORS WITH DISABILITIES

Legislation aimed at improving access for visitors with disabilities in Chicago means that all recently built structures have to provide disabled access; the newer they are, the stricter the rules. Many older buildings, including most hotels, have been converted to ensure they comply. Both airports are accessible, as are many CTA buses and El stations. For details log on to www.transitchicago.com or www.cityofchicago.org/disabilities.

Much of Chicago can be explored on foot. To travel between neighborhoods use the network of buses and El (elevated) trains, which travel above and below ground. El trains operate 24-hours a day. Best value over many journeys are the Visitor Pass tickets valid for 1–7 days (cost $5.75–$23). Buy them from the airport, CTA stations, from major museums and the Visitor Information center (for information ☎ 1-888/968-7282). Tokens, cash and multi-use plastic cards can also be used. Taxis wait outside hotels, conference halls and major El stations, or can be hailed.

● Using trains or buses at night can be dangerous.

● Metra commuter trains are best for visiting some areas (www.metrarail.com).

● For information on the El and buses: Chicago Transit Authority ☎ 888/968-7282; Metra ☎ 312/322-6900 or 312/322-6777.

THE EL

● Fare: $2.25 cash, $2 with card, plus 25¢ transfer. Transfer to a different line (or to a bus) within two hours: 25¢ (free within Loop). A second transfer within the same two hours is free. Children 7–11 ride for $1 cash, 85¢ with card, plus 15¢ transfer. Kids under age 6 travel free.

● Plastic transit cards are the simplest way to pay fares. Cash is an alternative. Cards are dispensed in exchange for cash from automated machines at train stations with a minimum value of $2. Replenish existing cards with more cash as needed at the same machines.

● Visitor passes valid for 1 day ($5.75), 3 days ($14), 7 days ($23) or 30 days ($86) permit unlimited rides on buses and trains. The pass activates the first time you use it and is good for the consecutive number of calendar days shown on the front of the pass. Order them before you arrive at the CTA website (www.transitchicago.com) or buy them at many hotels, Chicago visitor centers and O'Hare and Midway CTA stations.

- Many stations have only automatic ticket machines.
- Eight color-coded lines run through the city and converge on the Loop.
- On weekdays 6am–7pm, some trains stop only at alternate stations, plus all major stations. Station announcements will alert you to the change.
- Most trains run 24 hours; frequency is reduced on weekends and during the night. The Brown, Green and Orange Lines suspend service between roughly 2am and 5am.
- Some stations are closed weekends.

BUSES
- Fare: $2 with a transit card, $2.25 with cash. Transfer to a different route (or to the El) within two hours: 25¢. Second transfer as for the El.
- As for the El, plastic transit cards are the simplest way to pay fares. They are sold at some CTA train stations and Visitor Information centers.

SCHEDULE AND MAP INFORMATION
- CTA maps showing El and bus routes are available from El station fare booths.
- Bus routes are shown at stops.
- The CTA website (www.transitchicago.com) contains all schedules and maps and offers directions on how to get to popular tourist attractions.

TAXIS
- Fares are $2.25 for the first mile and $1.80 for each additional mile. The second additional passenger costs $1 and each additional passenger after that costs 50¢. Midway- and O'Hare-bound trips cost an extra $1 and there is a $1 surcharge whenever gas costs over $3 per gallon.
- Hotel, restaurant and nightclub staff will order a taxi on request; or you can phone Checker ☎ 312/243-2537; Flash ☎ 773/561-4444 or Yellow ☎ 312/829-4222.

GOING BY WATER

In spring and summer the Chicago Water Taxi (☎ 312/337-1446; www.chicagowatertaxi.com) offers a ferry service from 6.30am to, roughly, sundown. Catch it at one of four stops along the Chicago River: Madison Street, La Salle Street, Michigan Avenue and Chinatown. A single one-way ticket costs $2, $4 if going to Chinatown, or $4 all-day pass.

MAPPING CHICAGO

Most of Chicago is laid out on a grid system with ground zero at State, which runs north–south, and Madison, east–west, in the Loop. Each block number changes by 100 with eight blocks equaling roughly one mile (1.6km). For instance, 800 N. State Street means the location is eight blocks north of the baseline intersection, while 110 E. Madison lies on the second block east of it. Even number addresses belong to the north or west side of a street; odd numbers mean the location is on the south or east side of a street.

Essential Facts

TRAVEL INSURANCE

Travel insurance is essential for the US because of the astronomical cost of any kind of medical treatment. Check your insurance policy and buy a supplementary policy if needed. A minimum of $1 million medical cover is recommended. Choose a policy that also includes trip cancellation, baggage loss and document loss.

MONEY

Dollar bills (notes) come in denominations of $1, $5, $10, $20, $50 and $100; coins are 25¢ (a quarter), 10¢ (a dime), 5¢ (a nickel) and 1¢ (a penny).

5 dollars

10 dollars

50 dollars

100 dollars

CUSTOMS REGULATIONS

● Duty-free allowances include 1 liter of alcoholic spirits or wine (no one under 21 may bring alcohol into the US), 200 cigarettes or 100 cigars, and up to $100-worth of gifts.
● Some medication bought over the counter abroad may be prescription-only in the US and may be confiscated. Bring a doctor's certificate for essential medication.
● It is forbidden to bring food, seeds and plants into the US.

ELECTRICITY

● The electricity supply is 110 volts; 60 cycles AC current.
● US appliances use two-prong plugs. European appliances require an adaptor.

ETIQUETTE

● Smoking is banned in all public buildings, restaurants, bars and on public transportation.
● Tipping is voluntary, but the following are usually expected: 15 percent-plus in restaurants; 15–20 percent for taxis; $1 per bag for a hotel porter.

INTERNATIONAL NEWSAGENTS

● Overseas newspapers and magazines can be found at Barnes & Noble and Borders Books & Music stores.

MEDICAL TREATMENT

● For doctors, ask hotel staff or the Chicago Medical Society ☎ 312/670-2550.
● In an emergency go to a hospital with a 24-hour emergency room, such as Northwestern Memorial Hospital at 251 E. Huron Street ☎ 312/926-2000.
● The Chicago Dental Society ☎ 312/836-7300 will refer you to a dentist in your area.

MEDICINES

● Pharmacies are listed in *Yellow Pages*. Visitors from Europe will find many familiar medicines under unfamiliar names. Some

drugs available over the counter at home, are prescription-only in the US.

● If you use medication bring a supply (but note the warning in Customs Regulations, ▷ 120). If you intend to buy prescription drugs in the US, bring a note from your doctor.

● Late-night pharmacies in the city include two branches of Walgreen's ✉ 757 N. Michigan Avenue ☎ 312/664-8686; 641 N. Clark Street ☎ 312/587-0904 🕐 Both 24 hours.

MONEY MATTERS

● Most banks have ATMs, which accept credit cards registered in other countries that are linked to the Cirrus or Plus networks. Ensure your personal identification number is valid in the US: four- and six-figure numbers are usual.

● Credit cards are widely accepted.

● US dollar traveler's checks function like cash in most shops; $20 and $50 denominations are most useful. Seeking to exchange these (or foreign currency) at a bank can be difficult and commissions can be high.

● A 10.25 percent sales tax is added to marked retail prices, except on groceries and prescription drugs.

● A Chicago City Pass or a Go Chicago Card offer multiple discounts to major tourist destinations (www.gochicagocard.com or www.citypass.com).

NEWSPAPERS AND MAGAZINES

● Major daily newspapers are the *Chicago Tribune* and the tabloid *Chicago Sun-Times* (international, national and local stories).

● Best of several free weeklies is the *Chicago Reader*. The glossy *Time Out Chicago* covers the same ground for a fee at newsstands.

● Glossy monthly magazines such as the *Chicago* reflect the interests of well-heeled Chicagoans. The *Windy City Times* pitches to gays and lesbians.

● Free magazines such as *Where Chicago*, which can be found in hotel lobbies, are aimed at tourists.

TOURIST OFFICES

Visitor centers are inside the Chicago Water Works building ✉ 163 E. Pearson Avenue ☎ 312/744-2400, and at Chicago Cultural Center ✉ 77 E. Randolph Street ☎ 312/744-2400. Both are open daily but may close on holidays.

NATIONAL HOLIDAYS

● New Year's Day (Jan 1)
● Martin Luther King Day (third Mon in Jan)
● President's Day (third Mon in Feb)
● Memorial Day (last Mon in May)
● Independence Day (Jul 4)
● Labor Day (first Mon in Sep)
● Columbus Day (second Mon in Oct)
● Veteran's Day (Nov 11)
● Thanksgiving Day (fourth Thu in Nov)
● Christmas Day (Dec 25)

EMERGENCY PHONE NUMBERS

● Fire, police or ambulance ☎ 911 (no money required)
● Rape Crisis Hotline ☎ 888/293-2080

LOST AND FOUND

● O'Hare International Airport ☎ 773/686-2385
● Items lost in a cab: Department of Consumer Services ☎ 312/746-7100
● The El and buses: Chicago Transit Authority ☎ 888/968-7282; Metra ☎ 312/322-7819
🕔 Daily 7.45am–1am

RADIO AND TV

Radio
● Classical: WFMT 98.7FM
● Country: WUSN 99.5FM
● Jazz: WNUA 95.5FM
● National Public Radio: WBEZ 91.5FM
● News: WBBM 780AM
● R&B: WGCI 107.5FM
● Talk radio and local sports: WGN 720AM; WSCR 670AM

Television
● The main Chicago TV channels are 2 WBBM (CBS), 5 WMAQ (NBC), 7 WLS (ABC), 9 WGN (local WB affiliate), 11 WTTW (PBS), 32 WFLD (Fox).

OPENING HOURS

● Stores: Mon–Sat from 9 or 10 until 6 or 7. Most stores are also open Sun noon–6. Department stores and malls keep longer hours; bookshops may open in the evenings.
● Banks: Mon–Fri from 9–3, with some branches open later once a week.

POST OFFICES

● Minimum charges for sending a postcard overseas are 75¢ to Canada, 79¢ to Mexico, and 98¢ elsewhere.
● To find the nearest post office, look in the phone book or ask at your hotel. Most open Mon–Fri 8.30–5, Sat 8.30–1.

SENSIBLE PRECAUTIONS

● By day, the Loop and major areas of interest to visitors are relatively safe. Some tourist sights involve journeys through unwelcoming areas; be especially wary if traveling through the South Side and West Side. Discuss your itinerary with hotel staff and heed their advice.
● After dark, stay in established nightlife areas. River North and River West, Rush and Division streets, and Lake View/Wrigleyville are fairly safe if you use common-sense precautions. Public transportation is generally safe between these areas, but be cautious.
● Neighborhoods can change character within a few blocks. Stick to safe, busy streets.
● Carry shoulder bags strapped across your chest, and keep your wallet in your front trouser pocket or chest pocket. Keep your belongings within sight and within reach.
● Store valuables in your hotel's safe and never carry more money than you need.
● Lost traveler's checks are easy to replace— read the instructions when you buy them and keep the instructions handy (separate from the checks).
● Replacing a stolen passport is tricky and begins with a visit or phone call to your nearest consular office.
● Report any item stolen to the nearest police

precinct (see the phone book). It is unlikely that stolen goods will be recovered, but the police will fill in the forms your insurance company needs.

SOLO VISITORS
● Solo visitors, including women, are not unusual.
● Women may encounter unwanted attention and, after dark, should avoid being out alone when not in established nightlife areas. Wait for a cab inside a club or restaurant, or where staff can see you.

STUDENT VISITORS
● An International Student Identity Card (ISIC) reduces admission prices to many museums and other attractions.
● Anyone aged under 21 is forbidden to buy or drink alcohol and may be denied admission to some nightclubs.

TELEPHONES
● Public telephones are found in the street and in public buildings. Local calls cost 35¢.
● Calls from hotel rooms are usually more expensive than those from public phones.
● Many businesses have toll-free numbers, prefixed with 800, 866 or 888.
● Most US phones use touch-tone dialing, enabling callers to access extensions directly.
● To call Chicago from the UK dial 001 followed by the full number. To call the UK from Chicago dial 011-44 and omit the first zero from the area code.

TOILETS
● Most department stores, malls and hotel lobbies have adequate toilets.

TRAVELING WITH CHILDREN
Chicago is a destination that welcomes children. Classic sights like the Willis Tower Observatory, Navy Pier, Shedd Aquarium, Field Museum, Museum of Science and Industry and the Chicago Children's Museum delight all ages, but especially kids. Furthermore, adults don't have to sacrifice their own interests to those of a child. The Art Institute of Chicago runs an outstanding visitor's program for children; check their website (www.artic.edu) for a month-by-month guide to the activities. The Crown Fountain in Millennium Park is a popular spot for kids to play in summer in the water while families tour the grounds. When rest is required for little legs go passive sightseeing by riding the El or taking a water taxi.

CONSULATES		
Germany	✉ 676 N. Michigan Avenue, Suite 3200	☎ 312/202-0480
Ireland	✉ 400 N. Michigan Avenue, Suite 911	☎ 312/337-1868
UK	✉ 400 N. Michigan Avenue, Suite 1300	☎ 312/970-3800

Timeline

WINDY CITY

In 1893 Chicago hosted the World's Columbian Exposition. The hyperbole of business leaders caused one journalist to describe Chicago as "the windy city," an enduring epithet.

THE HAYMARKET RIOT

Heavy-handed police tactics in a series of labor disputes prompted a group of German-born anarchists to organize a protest rally on May 4, 1886, in Haymarket Square. A bomb thrown from the crowd exploded among the police lines; the explosion and the police use of firearms killed seven people and wounded 150. Seven anarchists received death sentences. In 1893, a full pardon was granted to three imprisoned anarchists, due to the lack of evidence linking any anarchists to the bomb.

1673 Missionary Jacques Marquette and explorer Louis Joliet discover the 1.5 mile (2.4km) Native-American portage trail linking the Mississippi River and the Great Lakes—the site of future Chicago.

1779–81 Trapper and trader Jean-Baptiste Point du Sable, a Haitian, becomes the first non-native settler.

1812 Fort Dearborn, one of several forts protecting trade routes, is attacked by Native Americans.

1830 Chicago is selected as the site of a canal linking the Great Lakes and the Mississippi.

1870 Chicago's population reaches 330,000 from 30,000 in 1850. Many arrivals are Irish, who find work building the railways.

1871 The Great Fire kills 300 people.

1894 A strike at the Pullman rail company unites black and white workers for the first time.

1906 Upton Sinclair's novel *The Jungle* focuses national attention on the conditions endured by workers in the notorious Union Stockyards.

1908 Chicago Cubs win baseball's World Series for a second successive year.

VISIT
CLARKE HOUSE
1836
CHICAGO'S OLDEST BUILDING
TURN RIGHT ON 18th STREET TO THE
PRAIRIE AVENUE HISTORIC DISTRICT TOUR CENTER

1914 With World War I, Chicago's black population increases further, as African-Americans from the Deep South move north to industrial jobs.

1919–33 Prohibition. Chicago's transport links make it a natural place for alcohol manufacture and distribution. Armed crime mobs thrive.

1950s In South Side clubs, rhythmic and electrified Chicago blues evolves.

1955 Richard J. Daley is elected mayor and dominates Chicago political life for 21 years.

1968 Police attack anti-Vietnam War protesters in Grant Park during the Democratic National Convention.

1974 Completion of Sears Tower (now Willis Tower), the world's tallest building until 1996.

1980s DJs at Chicago's Warehouse nightclub create house music.

1992 A collapsing wall causes the Chicago River to flood the Loop.

2005 The Chicago White Sox baseball team win the World Series.

2009 Illinois senator and Chicago resident Barack Obama is sworn in as the 44th President of the United States.

GANGSTERS

Intended to encourage sobriety and family life, Prohibition (1919–33) provided a great stimulus to organized crime. The exploits of Chicago-based gangsters such as Al Capone became legendary. Though depicted frequently on films and TV, shoot-outs between rival gangs were rare. An exception was the 1929 Valentine's Day Massacre, when Capone's gang eliminated their archrivals in a hail of machine-gun fire. Wealthy enough to bribe corruptible politicians and police, the gangsters seemed invincible, but the gangster era—though not necessarily the gangs—ended with Capone's imprisonment in 1931 and the repeal of Prohibition.

From left to right: directions to Clarke House; a baseball game in progress at Wrigley Field; an old copy of the Chicago Daily Tribune; *the Chicago skyline from the Willis Tower*

Index

INDEX

CITYPACK TOP 25
Chicago

WRITTEN BY Mick Sinclair
ADDITIONAL WRITING Elaine Glusac
UPDATED BY Mike Gerrard and Donna Dailey
COVER DESIGN AND DESIGN WORK Jacqueline Bailey
INDEXER Marie Lorimer
IMAGE RETOUCHING AND REPRO Sarah Montgomery and James Tims
PROJECT EDITOR Apostrophe S Limited
SERIES EDITOR Marie-Claire Jefferies

First published 1997
New edition 2007
Information verified and updated for 2011

Colour separation by AA Digital Department
Printed and bound by Leo Paper Products, China

A CIP catalogue record for this book is available from the British Library.

ISBN 978-0-7495-5086-8

Published by AA Publishing, a trading name of AA Media Limited, whose registered
office is Fanum House, Basing View, Basingstoke, Hampshire RG21 4EA. Registered
number 06112600.

A04202
Maps in this title produced from mapping © MAIRDUMONT / Falk Verlag 2011
and map data © Global Mapping (www.globalmapping.uk.com)
Transport map © Communicarta Ltd, UK

The Automobile Association wishes to thank the following photographers, companies and picture libraries for their assistance in the preparation of this book.

Abbreviations for the picture credits are as follows – (t) top; (b) bottom; (l) left; (r) right; (c) centre; (AA) AA World Travel Library

F/C Courtesy of John Hancock Tower; **B/C(i)** AA/P Wilson; **B/C(ii)** AA/C Sawyer; **B/C(iii)** AA/C Sawyer; **B/C(iv)** AA/P Wilson; **1** AA/C Sawyer; **2** AA/C Sawyer; **3** AA/C Sawyer; **4** AA/C Sawyer; **4c** AA/C Sawyer; **5t** AA/C Sawyer; **5b** AA/P Wilson; **6t** AA/C Sawyer; **6cl** AA/C Sawyer; **6ct** AA/P Wilson; **6bl** AA/C Sawyer; **6br** AA/C Sawyer; **7t** AA/C Sawyer; **7cl** AA/C Sawyer; **7cr** AA/C Sawyer; **7bl** AA/C Sawyer; **7bc** AA/C Sawyer; **7br** AA/C Sawyer; **8** AA/C Sawyer; **9** AA/C Sawyer; **10t** AA/C Sawyer; **10ct** AA/C Sawyer; **10c** AA/A Mockford & N Bonetti; **10cb** AA/C Sawyer; **10/11** AA/C Sawyer; **11t** AA/C Sawyer; **11ct** AA/C Sawyer; **11c** AA/C Sawyer; **11cb** AA/C Sawyer; **12t** AA/C Sawyer; **12b** AA/C Sawyer; **13t** AA/C Sawyer; **13ctt** AA/C Saywer; **13ct** AA/C Sawyer; **13c** AA/C Sawyer; **13cb** AA/C Sawyer; **13b** AA/C Sawyer; **14t** AA/C Sawyer; **14ctt** AA/C Sawyer; **14ct** AA/C Sawyer; **14c** AA/C Sawyer; **14cb** AA/C Sawyer; **14b** AA/C Sawyer; **15** AA/C Sawyer; **16t** AA/C Sawyer; **16ct** AA/C Sawyer; **16cb** AA/C Sawyer; **16b** AA/C Sawyer; **17t** AA/C Sawyer; **17ct** AA/C Sawyer; **17c** Digital Vision; **17cb** AA/C Sawyer; **17b** AA/C Sawyer; **18t** AA/C Sawyer; **18ct** AA/C Sawyer; **18c** AA/C Sawyer; **18cb** J Lindsey/Alamy; **18b** AA/C Sawyer; **19t** AA/C Sawyer; **19ct** AA/C Sawyer; **19c** AA/C Sawyer; **19cb** AA/C Sawyer; **19b** AA/C Sawyer; **20/21** AA/P Wilson; **24l** AA/C Sawyer; **24r** AA/C Sawyer; **25l** AA/C Sawyer; **25r** AA/C Sawyer; **26l** AA/C Sawyer; **26r** AA/C Sawyer; **27l** AA/C Sawyer; **27r** AA/C Sawyer; **28t** AA/C Sawyer; **28bl** Bloomberg via Getty Images; **28br** AA/C Sawyer; **29** AA/C Sawyer; **30t** AA/P Wilson; **30bl** AA/P Wilson; **30br** AA/P Wilson; **31t** AA/P Wilson; **31bl** Museum of Contemporary Art; **31br** AA/P Wilson; **32** AA/P Wilson; **33** AA/A Mockford & N Bonetti; **34** AA/C Sawyer; **35** Digital Vision; **36** AA/C Sawyer; **37** AA/C Sawyer; **38** AA/C Sawyer; **39** AA/C Sawyer; **42l** AA/P Wilson; **42/43t** AA/P Wilson; **42/43c** AA/P Wilson; **43cl** AA/P Wilson; **43cr** AA/P Wilson; **44** Art Institute of Chicago; **45** Art Institute of Chicago; **46t** AA/P Wilson; **46cl** AA/C Sawyer; **46cr** AA/P Wilson; **46/47** AA/C Sawyer; **48t** Shedd Aquarium; **48b** Shedd Aquarium; **49l** Shedd Aquarium; **49t** Shedd Aquarium; **50l** AA/C Sawyer; **50r** AA/C Sawyer; **51t** AA/P Wilson; **51bl** AA/P Wilson; **51br** AA/P Wilson; **52** AA/P Wilson; **53t** AA/Slide File; **53c** AA/C Sawyer; **54** Imagestate; **55** AA/C Sawyer; **58** Jonathan Daniel/Getty Images; **59l** AA/P Wilson; **59r** Chris McGrath/Getty Images; **60l** Signature Room at the 95th, Chicago; **60r** Signature at the 95th, Chicago; **61l** AA/C Sawyer; **61r** AA/C Sawyer; **62t** AA/C Sawyer; **62cl** AA/C Sawyer; **62cr** AA/C Sawyer; **63t** AA/C Sawyer; **63cl** AA/C Sawyer; **63cr** AA/C Sawyer; **64** AA/C Sawyer; **64/65t** AA/C Sawyer; **64/65c** AA/C Sawyer; **65** AA/C Sawyer; **66l** AA/C Sawyer; **66r** AA/P Wilson; **67l** AA/C Sawyer; **67c** AA/C Sawyer; **67r** AA/C Sawyer; **68l** AA/C Sawyer; **68c** AA/C Sawyer; **68r** AA/C Sawyer; **69t** AA/P Wilson; **69bl** Chicago Children's Museum; **69br** AA/P Wilson; **70t** AA/P Wilson; **70bl** International Museum of Surgical Sciences; **70br** AA/C Sawyer; **71t** AA/P Wilson; **71b** AA/P Wilson; **72t** AA/P Wilson; **72bl** AA/C Sawyer; **72br** AA/P Wilson; **73** AA/P Wilson; **74** AA/S McBride; **75** AA/M Chaplow; **76** Digital Vision; **77** AA/C Sawyer; **78** Photodisc; **79** AA/C Sawyer; **80** Photodisc; **81** AA/C Sawyer; **84l** AA/C Sawyer; **84r** AA/C Sawyer; **85l** AA/P Wilson; **85r** AA/P Wilson; **86l** AA/C Sawyer; **86r** AA/C Sawyer; **87l** AA/C Sawyer; **87r** Glessner House; **88l** Museum of Science and Industry; **88/89t** Museum of Science and Industry; **88c** Museum of Science and Industry; **88/89c** Museum of Science and Industry; **89t** Museum of Science and Industry; **89r** Museum of Science and Industry; **90t** AA/P Wilson; **90b** AA/C Sawyer; **91t** AA/P Wilson; **91bl** Smart Museum; **91br** AA/P Wilson; **92** AA/P Wilson; **93** AA/C Sawyer; **94** AA/C Sawyer; **95** AA/C Sawyer; **98** AA/C Sawyer; **99l** AA/C Sawyer; **99r** AA/C Sawyer; **100** AA/C Sawyer; **101** The Frank Lloyd Wright Preservation Trust – photographer Tim Long; **102t** AA/P Wilson; **102bl** AA/P Wilson; **102br** AA/C Sawyer; **103** AA/C Sawyer; **104** Digital Vision; **105** Photodisc; **106** AA/C Sawyer; **107** AA/C Sawyer; **108t** AA/C Sawyer; **108ct** AA/C Sawyer; **108c** AA/C Sawyer **108cb** AA/S McBride; **108b** Stockbyte Royalty Free; **109** AA/C Sawyer; **110** AA/C Sawyer; **111** AA/C Sawyer; **112** AA/C Sawyer; **113** AA/C Sawyer; **114** AA/C Sawyer; **115** AA/C Sawyer; **116** AA/C Sawyer; **117** AA/C Sawyer; **118** AA/C Sawyer; **119t** AA/C Sawyer; **119b** AA/C Sawyer; **120t** AA/C Sawyer; **120b** MRI Bankers' Guide; **121** AA/C Sawyer; **122t** AA/C Sawyer; **122b** AA/C Sawyer; **123t** AA/C Sawyer; **123b** AA/C Sawyer; **124t** AA/C Sawyer; **124bl** AA/P Wilson; **124br** AA/C Sawyer; **125t** AA/C Sawyer; **125bl** AA/P Wilson; **125br** AA/C Sawyer.

Every effort has been made to trace the copyright holders, and we apologise in advance for any unintentional omissions or errors. We would be please to apply any corrections in any following edition of this publication.